HELOC Paydown and Redraw Strategies

How to Reduce Interest While Preserving Future Access to Capital

By Joseph G. Correa

Published by Live Stronger Faster

This book is for educational and informational purposes only. The author and publisher are not engaged in rendering legal, financial, or other professional advice. Readers should consult a qualified professional before making any financial decisions.

First Edition

Table of Contents

Introduction

Home equity can be one of a homeowner's most valuable financial resources, but it becomes useful only when it is managed with discipline. A home equity line of credit, commonly called a HELOC, gives a qualified homeowner the ability to borrow against a portion of the equity accumulated in a property. Unlike a traditional loan that delivers one fixed amount at closing, a HELOC generally allows money to be borrowed, repaid, and borrowed again during an established draw period. This revolving structure creates valuable flexibility, but it also introduces a challenge: the same access that makes a HELOC useful can make it easy to carry a balance longer than intended. A successful strategy must therefore accomplish two objectives at the same time. It must reduce the outstanding balance and the interest charged on that balance while preserving enough available credit to support future needs and opportunities.

This book focuses on the relationship between paying down a HELOC and maintaining the ability to redraw funds. These two actions may appear to work against each other. Paying down the balance moves the homeowner toward lower debt and lower interest expense, while redrawing increases the balance and creates additional interest. However, when the line is managed intentionally, repayment and future access can work together. A homeowner may use surplus income to reduce the balance, rebuild available credit, and lower the amount on which interest is calculated. If a legitimate expense arises later, part of that restored borrowing capacity may be available again. The objective is not to create a permanent cycle of borrowing and repayment. It is to use the revolving structure as a controlled financial tool while steadily improving the homeowner's overall position.

A HELOC should not be viewed as extra income. The available credit shown on an account statement may feel similar to money in a savings account, but it is borrowed capital secured by the home. Every draw increases debt, creates an obligation to make payments, and places a portion of the homeowner's equity at risk. This distinction is central to every strategy discussed in the book. A person who treats the credit line as spendable wealth may gradually convert home equity into lifestyle debt. A person who treats it as conditional borrowing capacity is more likely to evaluate each draw according to its purpose, cost, repayment source, and effect on long-term goals.

The potential benefit of paying down a HELOC begins with the way interest is commonly calculated. HELOC interest is generally based on the outstanding balance, often using an average daily balance or a similar method described in the loan agreement. Reducing principal sooner can therefore reduce the balance subject to interest. Even when the scheduled payment is interest-only during the draw period, the borrower may be allowed to make additional principal payments without waiting for the repayment period to begin. Those voluntary payments can decrease current interest expense and restore part of the line's available credit, assuming the lender continues to permit additional draws and the account remains in good standing.

The phrase "paydown and redraw" may sound like a complicated banking technique, but the underlying concept is straightforward. When a borrower repays principal on a revolving credit line, the available credit may increase by the amount of principal repaid. If the borrower later needs funds and remains within the draw period, that credit may be accessible again. For example, a homeowner with a $100,000 credit limit and a $60,000 balance has approximately $40,000 of unused credit. If the homeowner pays $10,000 toward principal, the balance may fall to $50,000 and available credit may rise to approximately $50,000. If $5,000 is later redrawn for an approved purpose, the balance may return to $55,000. Interest would then be based on the changing balance rather than on the original amount borrowed.

This flexibility can be valuable for households with uneven income. Business owners, commission-based professionals, seasonal workers, real estate investors, and households receiving periodic bonuses may not earn the same amount every month. A rigid financial plan based only on equal monthly payments may fail to use periods of strong cash flow efficiently. A paydown strategy can direct a portion of larger income deposits toward HELOC principal, reducing the balance during stronger months. If income later slows or a planned expense occurs, the borrower may retain access to part of the line rather than keeping every available dollar idle in a checking account. The decision must still account for the need to maintain dependable cash reserves because a HELOC is not guaranteed to remain available under every circumstance.

That last point is critical. Paying money into a HELOC is not identical to depositing money in an insured bank account. Cash held in checking or savings belongs to the account holder and can ordinarily be withdrawn subject to the account's terms. Available HELOC credit belongs to the lender until it is advanced to the borrower. The lender may freeze, suspend, reduce, or close the line under circumstances permitted by the agreement and applicable law. A substantial decline in the property's value, a deterioration in the borrower's financial condition, payment problems, suspected fraud, or the expiration of the draw period may affect access. For this reason, homeowners should not place every dollar of emergency savings into a HELOC under the assumption that it can always be redrawn.

A sound paydown plan begins by separating liquidity from borrowing capacity. Liquidity is money the household already owns and can use without creating debt. Borrowing capacity is money that may be available from a lender under specified conditions. Both can support financial stability, but they are not interchangeable. A homeowner may decide to maintain a minimum cash reserve for immediate emergencies while applying cash above that minimum toward the HELOC. The correct reserve amount depends on income stability, household expenses, insurance deductibles, health considerations, property condition, employment risk, and the remaining draw period. The strategy should protect the household from having to redraw for every small expense while still preventing excessive cash from sitting unused as a large HELOC balance generates interest.

The timing of payments also matters. Many borrowers focus exclusively on the required payment shown on the monthly statement. That payment keeps the account current, but it may do little or nothing to reduce principal during an interest-only draw period. A borrower who wants the balance to decline must distinguish between interest owed and principal voluntarily repaid. Sending additional money without understanding how the lender applies it can also cause confusion. Some lenders may treat extra funds as principal reduction, while others may first apply payments to accrued interest, fees, or other amounts. Borrowers need to review statements and payment instructions to verify that additional payments produce the intended result.

An effective strategy also requires a clear rule for future draws. Without such a rule, the borrower may repeatedly pay down the line and then restore the balance through discretionary spending. The account may appear active and well managed while the principal remains unchanged year after year. A practical redraw standard considers whether the expense is necessary, whether it protects or improves the household's financial position, whether less expensive funding is available, and how the new balance will be repaid. A draw for a necessary roof replacement, a temporary business expense supported by expected receivables, or a carefully analyzed property renovation is fundamentally different from using home equity to finance recurring consumption that the monthly budget cannot support.

Every redraw should have a repayment source identified before the money is borrowed. That source might be monthly surplus income, a scheduled bonus, business receivables, the sale of an asset, reimbursement proceeds, or rental income. The repayment source should be reasonably dependable and should have a realistic timeline. Simply expecting that "future income will be higher" is not a repayment plan. If the anticipated funds do not arrive, the borrower may be left with a larger variable-rate balance and no clear way to reduce it. The line then stops functioning as a temporary liquidity tool and begins operating as long-term debt.

Interest-rate risk is another major part of HELOC management. Many HELOCs have variable rates composed of an index, such as the prime rate, plus a lender's margin. If the index rises, the borrower's interest rate and required payment can rise even when no additional money is borrowed. A strategy that appears affordable at one rate may become uncomfortable after several increases. Paying down principal can help control this risk because the rate applies to a smaller balance. However, repeatedly redrawing the amount repaid can erase that protection. The borrower should therefore evaluate not only the current payment but also the payment that could result from a higher rate.

The transition from the draw period to the repayment period deserves equal attention. During the draw period, the borrower may be permitted to borrow repeatedly and may have relatively low minimum payments, especially if payments are based primarily on interest. When the repayment period begins, access to additional funds usually ends, and the outstanding balance must be repaid over the remaining term. This change can produce a significant payment increase because the borrower must begin paying principal in addition to interest. A paydown and redraw strategy that ignores the end of the draw period can create a serious cash-flow problem. The closer the account moves toward that deadline, the more conservative the borrower should generally become about new draws.

A homeowner should know exactly how much time remains in the draw period and create milestones for reducing the balance before repayment begins. If five years remain, for example, the borrower might establish annual principal targets rather than waiting until the final year. If the balance is repeatedly restored after each paydown, the homeowner may reach the conversion date with nearly as much debt as at the beginning. A more disciplined approach can gradually lower the maximum balance the household is willing to carry. The line may remain available, but the internal limit established by the borrower becomes smaller as the end of the draw period approaches.

The purpose of preserving access to capital is not to justify staying in debt indefinitely. Preserved access can provide flexibility while the homeowner is executing a broader financial plan. It may allow a business owner to manage short-term timing differences between expenses and revenue. It may help a property owner address urgent repairs without liquidating investments at an unfavorable time. It may support a planned renovation when the cost and repayment source have been analyzed. Yet access has value only when it is combined with restraint. The best available credit is often credit that remains unused until a sufficiently important need arises.

This book will also address the difference between productive and unproductive borrowing. Productive borrowing is not automatically safe, and unproductive borrowing is not always obvious. A project described as an "investment" can still lose money, exceed its budget, or fail to generate the expected return. A home improvement may increase comfort without increasing the property's market value by an equal amount. A business draw may support expansion but also expose the homeowner's residence to business risk. Each use must be evaluated on its own economics rather than justified by a broad label. The central question is whether the probable benefit is sufficient to compensate for the interest, fees, risk, and reduced equity created by the draw.

Careful recordkeeping supports better decisions. A homeowner should be able to identify the date, amount, purpose, interest rate, and planned repayment source for each major draw. This creates a clear picture of how the line is being used and prevents unrelated expenses from becoming one indistinguishable balance. It can also reveal whether the strategy is accomplishing its stated goal. If the balance trends downward over six or twelve months, interest expense decreases, and available credit improves without weakening cash reserves, the plan may be working. If the balance remains flat or rises despite frequent payments, the household may be redrawing too aggressively or operating without enough monthly surplus.

A monthly review can transform the HELOC from a passive obligation into an actively managed account. The review should examine the current balance, available credit, interest rate, interest charged, minimum payment, additional principal paid, new draws, remaining draw period, and emergency savings. The borrower can then compare these figures with previously established targets. Small deviations can be corrected before they become large problems. A rising balance may lead to a temporary halt on nonessential draws. A declining cash reserve may require smaller extra principal payments. A rate increase may justify directing more surplus toward the HELOC or comparing other repayment alternatives.

The strategy must also fit with the rest of the borrower's debts. Paying down a HELOC may not always be the first priority if the household has credit cards, personal loans, tax obligations, or other debts carrying higher rates or more severe consequences. At the same time, the fact that another debt has a higher rate does not eliminate the risk of a HELOC, because the home secures it. The borrower must compare interest costs, tax treatment, required payments, maturity dates, collateral risk, and available liquidity. Preserving HELOC capacity while expensive unsecured debt continues to grow may be inefficient, but using home equity to pay unsecured debt without correcting the spending pattern can place the home at greater risk.

Behavior is ultimately as important as mathematics. A spreadsheet may show that moving surplus money into the HELOC reduces interest, but the result depends on whether the borrower leaves the balance lower. If restored availability encourages additional spending, the theoretical savings may never materialize. Some borrowers benefit from strict redraw categories, a waiting period before nonemergency draws, separate accounts for recurring expenses, and a written balance-reduction target. Others may determine that a revolving line creates too much temptation and that a fixed repayment structure would better support their goals. The strongest strategy is the one the borrower can follow consistently.

Throughout this book, the emphasis will remain on intentional control. You will learn how to establish a safe cash-reserve floor, calculate the effect of principal reductions, organize irregular income, create rules for redrawing, monitor variable-rate exposure, prepare for the end of the draw period, and measure whether your balance is actually moving in the right direction. You will also examine common mistakes, including counting available credit as savings, using repeated draws to cover structural budget deficits, applying every dollar of cash to the line, and assuming that future access is guaranteed.

The goal is not to keep a HELOC active forever, nor is it necessarily to eliminate it as quickly as possible regardless of every other consideration. The goal is to manage the balance, cost, liquidity, and risk as parts of one coordinated plan. For some homeowners, that may mean aggressive principal reduction while maintaining a substantial emergency reserve. For others, it may mean using seasonal income to reduce the balance and permitting narrowly defined redraws during predictable low-income periods. Still others may choose to stop borrowing entirely as the end of the draw period approaches. The appropriate path depends on the borrower's income, expenses, objectives, risk tolerance, and loan terms.

Home equity represents years of mortgage payments, property maintenance, market changes, and financial commitment. A HELOC can make a portion of that value accessible, but accessibility should never be confused with affordability. Every draw should serve a defined purpose, and every paydown should move the homeowner toward a stronger position. When those principles guide the account, a HELOC can provide flexibility without becoming a permanent drain on cash flow. The chapters ahead will show you how to build that discipline into a practical paydown and redraw system—one designed to reduce interest, protect liquidity, preserve future choices, and keep control of your home equity firmly within your long-term financial plan.

[illegible]

A home equity line of credit differs from most forms of mortgage debt because it is designed to operate as a revolving source of funds. When a homeowner receives a traditional mortgage, the entire loan amount is generally advanced at closing, and the borrower repays that balance through scheduled monthly payments. A HELOC normally provides a maximum credit limit, but the borrower pays interest only on the portion that has actually been drawn. During the draw period, principal that is repaid may become available to borrow again. Understanding this cycle of borrowing, repayment, restored availability, and possible redrawing is the foundation of every effective HELOC paydown strategy.

The first step is to distinguish among the credit limit, outstanding balance, and available credit. The credit limit is the maximum amount the lender has approved for the line, subject to the terms of the agreement and to any future restrictions imposed by the lender. The outstanding balance is the amount currently owed. Available credit is generally the difference between the credit limit and the outstanding balance, although pending transactions, accrued interest, fees, minimum draw requirements, or lender restrictions may affect the exact amount available. If a homeowner has a $100,000 HELOC limit and owes $40,000, the homeowner generally has approximately $60,000 of available credit. The homeowner does not owe that $60,000; it represents additional borrowing that may be borrowed.

This distinction is important because available credit can create a false sense of financial security. A homeowner may look at the unused balance and believe that the money is available for future emergencies. However, that

Chapter 1

Comprehending the HELOC Paydown-and-Redraw Cycle

A home equity line of credit is different from most forms of mortgage debt because it is designed to operate as a revolving source of capital. When a homeowner receives a traditional mortgage, the entire loan amount is generally advanced at closing, and the borrower repays that balance through scheduled monthly payments. A HELOC normally provides a maximum credit limit, but the borrower pays interest only on the portion that has actually been drawn. During the draw period, principal that is repaid may become available to borrow again. Understanding this cycle of borrowing, repayment, restored availability, and possible redrawing is the foundation of every effective HELOC paydown strategy.

The first step is to distinguish among the credit limit, outstanding balance, and available credit. The credit limit is the maximum amount the lender has approved for the line, subject to the terms of the agreement and any future restriction imposed by the lender. The outstanding balance is the amount currently owed. Available credit is generally the difference between the credit limit and the outstanding balance, although pending transactions, accrued interest, fees, minimum-draw requirements, or lender restrictions may affect the exact amount available. If a homeowner has a $150,000 HELOC limit and owes $90,000, the line may show approximately $60,000 of available credit. The homeowner does not own that $60,000; it represents additional money that may be borrowed.

This distinction is important because an available credit amount can create a false sense of financial security. A homeowner may look at the line and believe that $60,000 is waiting for future emergencies. However, that amount is not the same as $60,000 held in a bank account. It is conditional borrowing capacity secured by the home. If the homeowner draws the money, the outstanding balance increases, interest begins accumulating, and the amount of unused credit falls. If the lender freezes or reduces the line under circumstances permitted by the HELOC agreement, some or all of the unused capacity may no longer be accessible. Available credit can supplement a financial plan, but it should not completely replace cash reserves.

During the draw period, many HELOCs allow the borrower to make payments and then reuse the principal that has been repaid. Suppose a homeowner owes $90,000 on a $150,000 line and sends a $15,000 principal payment. After the payment is processed and applied, the balance may fall to $75,000 while the available credit may increase from approximately $60,000 to approximately $75,000. If the homeowner later draws $10,000 for a necessary expense, the balance may rise to $85,000 and the available credit may fall to approximately $65,000. This movement is the basic paydown-and-redraw cycle.

The opportunity to redraw repaid principal can make additional HELOC payments feel less permanent than additional payments made on a closed-end mortgage. When a homeowner pays extra principal on a standard first mortgage, the loan balance declines, but the borrower generally cannot retrieve that money without refinancing, obtaining another loan, or selling the property. With a HELOC that remains open and within its draw period, principal payments may restore borrowing availability. This feature can encourage homeowners to direct surplus income toward the balance because they may still retain conditional access to the repaid amount. Nevertheless, the borrower must verify the lender's specific rules because not every line operates in exactly the same way.

A successful strategy starts with understanding how interest is generated. HELOC interest is typically based on the outstanding principal balance and a variable annual interest rate. Many lenders calculate interest using a daily periodic rate. The annual rate is divided by 365, and that daily rate is applied to the balance for each day in the billing cycle. Consequently, reducing the balance earlier can create more interest savings than waiting until the end of the month to make the same principal payment. The exact calculation depends on the agreement, but the general principle remains consistent: fewer dollars outstanding for fewer days ordinarily produce less interest.

For example, assume a borrower owes $80,000 at an annual rate of 9.50 percent. A simplified estimate of one month's interest can be calculated by multiplying $80,000 by 9.50 percent and dividing the result by twelve. That produces estimated monthly interest of approximately $633.33. If the borrower reduces the principal to $65,000, the simplified monthly interest estimate falls to approximately $514.58. The $15,000 principal reduction therefore lowers estimated interest by approximately $118.75 per month while the balance remains lower and the rate remains unchanged. Over twelve months, the simplified savings would be approximately $1,425.

Those savings disappear gradually or immediately if the borrower redraws the principal. If the homeowner repays $15,000 but redraws the entire $15,000 a week later, the balance returns to its previous level and most of the anticipated long-term savings are lost. There may still be a small benefit for the days during which the balance was lower, but that temporary reduction does not create the same result as keeping the principal out of the line for several months. A paydown should therefore be evaluated according to both the amount repaid and the length of time that amount is expected to remain undrawn.

This is why the purpose of a paydown must be established before money is transferred. A homeowner may make an additional principal payment for several possible reasons. The objective may be to reduce interest, create more available credit, prepare for the end of the draw period, lower exposure to a variable rate, or temporarily place irregular income against the balance. Each purpose can be valid, but it leads to a different decision about whether and when the money should be redrawn. A payment intended to eliminate debt should ordinarily remain in the line permanently. A payment intended to manage seasonal cash flow may be followed by a planned redraw, but that redraw should be limited and supported by a specific repayment source.

Homeowners with irregular income may find the revolving structure particularly useful. A business owner may receive $25,000 during a strong month but need part of that money for operating expenses several months later. Instead of leaving the entire amount in a checking account while a large HELOC balance accumulates interest, the owner may keep an appropriate cash reserve and apply a carefully selected portion toward the line. If some of that money is required later, the owner may redraw it during the draw period. While the balance is lower, the borrower may save interest. The effectiveness of this approach depends on maintaining adequate cash, preserving access to the line, and resisting draws that were not included in the original plan.

A commission-based worker could follow a similar method. Strong commission months may generate more income than the household needs for current expenses. Rather than allowing the surplus to become absorbed by discretionary spending, the borrower can establish a rule that directs a percentage of each commission toward HELOC principal. During weaker months, the household relies first on its cash reserve and normal budget adjustments. The HELOC is redrawn only if necessary and only for an amount that can reasonably be repaid from future commissions. This creates a controlled system instead of an improvised cycle of borrowing whenever the checking-account balance becomes uncomfortable.

A HELOC paydown plan should include a cash-reserve floor. This is the minimum amount of money the household will keep outside the line regardless of how much interest might be saved by making a larger payment. The reserve protects against events in which immediate cash is required or the lender restricts additional borrowing. A household with stable salaries, strong insurance coverage, low fixed expenses, and several income sources may be comfortable with a different reserve than a household dependent on one variable income, facing major property repairs, or approaching the end of the HELOC draw period. The reserve should be based on realistic household risk rather than on the desire to maximize interest savings at any cost.

Once the reserve floor is established, the homeowner can define the amount available for principal reduction. Suppose a household has $40,000 in cash and determines that it needs to retain $25,000 for emergencies, insurance deductibles, irregular bills, and income interruptions. The remaining $15,000 could potentially be applied to the HELOC. This does not mean the entire $15,000 must be paid immediately. The homeowner may choose to transfer $10,000 and keep an additional $5,000 buffer until upcoming expenses become clearer. A slightly smaller payment that leaves the household financially comfortable may be more sustainable than an aggressive payment that forces a redraw within a few weeks.

The homeowner must also distinguish between the required monthly payment and an actual reduction of principal. During an interest-only draw period, the minimum payment may cover primarily or exclusively the interest accrued during the billing cycle. Paying that amount keeps the account current but may leave the principal balance almost unchanged. A borrower who wants to reduce the balance must pay more than the interest and any applicable fees. Statements should be reviewed carefully to confirm how much of each payment was applied to interest and how much reduced principal.

When making an extra payment, the borrower should verify the lender's payment process. Some servicing systems allow the homeowner to identify an additional principal amount, while others automatically apply any amount above the required payment to principal after satisfying accrued interest and fees. The borrower should not assume that a payment has produced the intended balance reduction until the transaction appears on the account. Reviewing the next statement or online balance can confirm that principal declined and available credit was restored.

An instructional paydown system can be organized around three internal categories even though the money remains part of one HELOC balance. The first category is permanent paydown, representing principal the homeowner intends never to redraw. The second category is temporary paydown, representing money applied to reduce interest but potentially needed for a known future expense. The third category is restored contingency capacity, representing available credit reserved for a significant emergency. These internal distinctions help prevent every dollar of restored availability from being treated as freely spendable money.

Permanent paydown should move the borrower toward a lower long-term balance. If the homeowner permanently repays $1,000 per month, the balance should decline by approximately $12,000 over a year before considering new interest, fees, or unrelated transactions. Temporary paydown may produce interest savings, but it does not necessarily reduce debt permanently if the money is later redrawn. Contingency capacity may never be used, and that is a successful outcome rather than a missed opportunity. The purpose of available credit is to preserve flexibility, not to create an obligation to borrow.

Every planned redraw should answer four questions. The homeowner should know why the money is needed, how much must be borrowed, when the draw will occur, and which income source will repay it. If any of those answers is unclear, the borrower should reconsider the transaction. A planned $8,000 draw for a roof repair supported by a written estimate and a defined repayment schedule is substantially different from a series of small draws used to cover ordinary spending. The first is a specific capital need. The second may indicate that recurring expenses exceed recurring income.

Repeated redrawing for groceries, utilities, entertainment, subscriptions, or routine bills is a warning sign unless the use is part of a short, clearly defined income interruption. When a household depends on the HELOC to pay normal expenses month after month, the line is no longer serving mainly as a flexible capital resource. It is funding a structural budget deficit. Because the debt is secured by the home, allowing routine spending to accumulate on the line can transform a manageable cash-flow issue into a significant home-equity risk.

The borrower should establish an internal borrowing limit that may be lower than the limit approved by the lender. A bank may approve a $200,000 HELOC, but the homeowner may decide never to allow the balance to exceed $120,000. After paying the balance down to $95,000, the homeowner would have $105,000 of lender-approved availability but only $25,000 of self-approved borrowing capacity. This internal limit adds discipline and prevents the lender's maximum approval from becoming the household's spending target.

The internal limit can be reduced over time. If a homeowner begins the year with a $100,000 balance, the first annual target might be to keep the balance below $90,000 after all permitted redraws. The next target might be $80,000. This approach allows controlled use of the line while still requiring measurable progress. If the balance ends every year at approximately the same level, the borrower may be making frequent payments without achieving permanent debt reduction.

The remaining draw period must influence the strategy. A borrower with eight years left in the draw period may have more flexibility than a borrower with only one year remaining. As the end of the draw period approaches, the homeowner generally needs to preserve more cash, reduce new borrowing, and prepare for principal-and-interest payments. Money paid into the line near the end of the draw period should not be assumed to remain available for redrawing after the account converts to repayment status. The loan agreement and lender communications should be reviewed well before the transition date.

Variable-rate exposure provides another reason to reduce principal. If the rate increases, interest charges rise even when the borrower makes no new draws. A $100,000 balance at 8 percent produces a simplified annual interest expense of approximately $8,000, while the same balance at 10 percent produces approximately $10,000. Reducing the balance to $70,000 limits the effect of the rate increase because the higher rate applies to fewer dollars. The borrower cannot control the index used to set the rate, but the borrower can influence the balance exposed to that rate.

The most effective paydown-and-redraw strategy is not necessarily the one that sends the largest possible payment to the HELOC. It is the one that produces consistent balance reduction without destabilizing the household. A plan that saves $200 in interest but causes the borrower to rely on credit cards for an unexpected expense may be counterproductive. The HELOC must be evaluated as one part of the homeowner's complete financial position, including cash reserves, other debts, income reliability, upcoming expenses, insurance coverage, and long-term goals.

At the end of each month, the homeowner should review the beginning balance, total draws, interest charged, fees, required payment, additional principal paid, ending balance, available credit, cash reserves, and time remaining in the draw period. These figures reveal whether the strategy is working. A declining ending balance and stable cash reserve generally indicate progress. A rising balance, frequent unplanned draws, or a shrinking reserve indicate that the rules need to be adjusted.

Understanding the paydown-and-redraw cycle provides the homeowner with a practical framework for managing home equity. Repaying principal can lower interest and restore available credit, but restored credit should not be mistaken for earned income or personal savings. Redrawing may be appropriate when it serves a defined purpose and is supported by a dependable repayment source. The ultimate objective is to use the HELOC's flexibility while ensuring that the balance, interest expense, and risk move in a controlled direction.

Practical Math Example: Building and Measuring a Paydown-and-Redraw Plan

Consider a homeowner named Daniel who has a HELOC with a $180,000 credit limit. His current outstanding balance is $120,000, which means he has approximately $60,000 of available credit. The line has a variable annual interest rate of 9.60 percent, and six years remain in the draw period. Daniel's minimum payment during the current draw period is based primarily on accrued interest, so making only the minimum payment will not materially reduce the principal.

Daniel has $42,000 in checking and savings. His essential household expenses average $7,000 per month, and his income varies because he owns a consulting business. After reviewing his income reliability, property expenses, insurance deductibles, and family obligations, Daniel decides to maintain a cash-reserve floor of $28,000. This amount represents four months of essential expenses. The difference between his total cash and his reserve floor is $14,000, which may be available for a HELOC principal payment.

Daniel does not immediately transfer the entire $14,000. He expects to pay approximately $3,000 in annual insurance premiums within the next two months, and he wants a small amount of flexibility above his formal reserve. He therefore chooses to make an initial $10,000 principal payment and leave $32,000 in cash. After the payment is processed, his HELOC balance falls from $120,000 to $110,000. His available credit increases from approximately $60,000 to approximately $70,000.

Before the payment, Daniel's simplified monthly interest estimate was calculated by multiplying the $120,000 balance by the 9.60 percent annual rate and dividing by twelve. The result was $960 per month. After the

$10,000 principal reduction, the simplified estimate becomes $880 per month because $110,000 multiplied by 9.60 percent and divided by twelve equals $880. If Daniel keeps the balance at $110,000 for a full year and the interest rate does not change, the $10,000 payment will save approximately $80 per month, or $960 over twelve months.

The actual HELOC calculation may use the daily balance rather than this simplified monthly formula. To estimate the daily effect, Daniel divides the 9.60 percent annual rate by 365. The resulting daily periodic rate is approximately 0.026301 percent. Interest on a $120,000 balance is approximately $31.56 per day, while interest on a $110,000 balance is approximately $28.93 per day. The $10,000 paydown therefore saves approximately $2.63 for every day the balance remains lower.

If Daniel leaves the $10,000 in the HELOC for 90 days, the estimated interest savings attributable to that payment would be approximately $236.70. This is found by multiplying the approximate daily savings of $2.63 by 90 days. If he leaves the balance lower for 180 days, the estimated savings increase to approximately $473.40. If the principal remains undrawn for an entire 365-day year, the estimated savings are approximately $959.95, which is close to the $960 result produced by the simplified annual calculation.

Three months later, Daniel's business needs $6,000 to purchase equipment required for a signed client project. The client contract is expected to produce a $15,000 payment within 60 days. Before using the HELOC, Daniel compares the draw with his established rules. The expense has a specific purpose, the exact amount is known, the expected revenue is documented by a signed contract, and there is a defined source for repaying the draw. He therefore approves the transaction within his personal financial system.

When Daniel draws $6,000, the HELOC balance rises from $110,000 to $116,000. Available credit falls from approximately $70,000 to approximately $64,000. His simplified monthly interest estimate rises to $928 because $116,000 multiplied by 9.60 percent and divided by twelve equals $928. Although this is $48 more than the estimated interest at the $110,000 balance, it is still $32 less than the $960 monthly estimate associated with his original $120,000 balance.

Daniel does not treat the $15,000 client payment as guaranteed until it is received. He retains his $28,000 reserve and does not schedule other optional spending based on the expected revenue. Sixty days later, the client pays the invoice. Daniel sets aside $3,000 for business taxes and $2,000 for upcoming operating costs. From the remaining $10,000, he uses $6,000 to repay the equipment draw and sends another $2,000 as permanent principal reduction. The remaining $2,000 stays in the business account as additional working capital.

After this payment, the HELOC balance falls from $116,000 to $108,000. The original $6,000 redraw has been completely repaid, and the additional $2,000 payment moves the balance below the previous low point of $110,000. Available credit increases to approximately $72,000. Daniel's simplified monthly interest estimate now falls to $864 because $108,000 multiplied by 9.60 percent and divided by twelve equals $864.

Compared with the original $120,000 balance, Daniel is now carrying $12,000 less principal. At the same 9.60 percent annual rate, the estimated annual interest difference is $1,152. This amount is calculated by multiplying the $12,000 reduction by 9.60 percent. The estimated monthly difference is $96. Daniel has also preserved $32,000 in personal cash, maintained working capital in his business, financed a revenue-producing expense, repaid the related draw, and achieved a permanent reduction in HELOC principal.

Daniel next creates a twelve-month paydown target. He wants to finish the year with a balance of no more than $100,000 after accounting for any approved redraws. His current balance is $108,000, so he needs an additional net principal reduction of $8,000. There are eight months left in his plan. Dividing $8,000 by eight produces a target of $1,000 in permanent principal reduction per month.

Daniel's required interest payment is not included in that $1,000 target. At the current $108,000 balance and 9.60 percent rate, his simplified interest estimate is $864 for the next month. If he wants to reduce principal by $1,000, his total payment for that month must be approximately $1,864, assuming no fees, new draws, rate changes, or differences caused by the lender's daily interest calculation. Paying only $1,000 would not reduce principal by the full amount because much of the payment would first be used to satisfy accrued interest.

During the following month, Daniel receives enough income to make a total payment of $2,364. Approximately $864 covers estimated interest, leaving approximately $1,500 to reduce principal. His new balance becomes approximately $106,500. Because he exceeded his $1,000 principal target by $500, he is slightly ahead of schedule. However, he does not automatically reduce the next month's goal. He records the extra $500 as progress toward the year-end target while continuing to aim for consistent reductions.

In the next month, Daniel encounters a $2,500 air-conditioning repair. He first evaluates whether the expense should come from cash or the HELOC. His cash balance is $31,000 after paying the insurance premiums anticipated earlier. Using $2,500 of cash would reduce the balance to $28,500, only $500 above his required reserve floor. He decides to pay $1,000 from cash and draw $1,500 from the HELOC. This allows him to complete the necessary repair while keeping his cash balance at $30,000.

The $1,500 draw increases the HELOC balance from approximately $106,500 to $108,000. Daniel immediately creates a three-month repayment schedule of $500 per month in addition to his regular $1,000 permanent principal target. For each of the next three months, his goal is therefore to reduce principal by $1,500. At a $108,000 balance and an estimated $864 monthly interest charge, the first payment would need to be approximately $2,364 to achieve that combined principal reduction.

If Daniel follows the plan for the full three months and makes no additional draws, he will reduce principal by approximately $4,500. Of that amount, $1,500 repays the air-conditioning draw and $3,000 advances his permanent paydown target. His balance would fall from approximately $108,000 to approximately $103,500. The emergency repair would be fully absorbed into the plan without permanently reversing his earlier progress.

Suppose Daniel then pays another $1,000 of principal in each of the next four months. This creates an additional $4,000 reduction and brings the estimated balance from $103,500 to $99,500. He finishes the year $500 below his maximum target of $100,000. Compared with the original $120,000 balance, he has achieved a net principal reduction of $20,500 despite making two redraws during the year.

At a constant annual rate of 9.60 percent, a $120,000 balance carries simplified annual interest of approximately $11,520. A $99,500 balance carries simplified annual interest of approximately $9,552. The difference is approximately $1,968 per year, or $164 per month, if the ending balance and rate remain unchanged. Daniel has also increased his approximate available credit from $60,000 at the beginning of the plan to $80,500 at the end.

The $80,500 of available credit does not become part of Daniel's spending budget. His internal maximum balance is now $110,000, even though the lender permits borrowing up to the $180,000 limit. With a $99,500 outstanding balance, Daniel has only $10,500 of self-approved borrowing capacity. The remaining lender-approved availability is treated as restricted contingency capacity. This internal limit protects the progress he has made and prevents the restored credit from encouraging unnecessary borrowing.

Daniel's example demonstrates why a paydown-and-redraw strategy must be measured according to net results. During the year, he repaid principal, borrowed for business equipment, repaid that business draw, borrowed part of the cost of an emergency repair, and then repaid that draw according to a defined schedule. Looking only at individual transactions might make the account appear highly active. The important result is that the balance declined from $120,000 to approximately $99,500 while cash reserves remained protected.

If Daniel had repaid $10,000 at the beginning of the year and then used the restored availability for vacations, entertainment, and routine expenses, the mathematical outcome would have been very different. A complete redraw of the $10,000 would have returned the balance to $120,000. Additional discretionary draws could have pushed it even higher. The original principal payment would then have provided only temporary interest savings rather than permanent improvement.

The practical lesson is that a HELOC paydown does not become successful merely because the account balance falls for a few days or weeks. The

strategy succeeds when the balance remains lower over time, redraws are limited to defined purposes, each redraw has a repayment source, and the household retains adequate cash. Daniel's progress came from combining mathematical discipline with behavioral rules. He did not confuse available credit with savings, he did not send his entire cash reserve to the lender, and he did not permit temporary borrowing to erase his long-term target.

A homeowner can apply the same process by recording the original balance, current rate, available credit, reserve floor, planned principal payment, expected redraws, and year-end balance target. Each month, actual results can be compared with the plan. If the ending balance is above the target, the homeowner can reduce new borrowing, increase principal payments, extend the repayment schedule, or revise spending. If the balance is below the target but the cash reserve has become too small, the homeowner may need to slow additional payments until liquidity is restored.

The calculations do not need to be complicated to be useful. The homeowner can estimate monthly interest by multiplying the balance by the annual rate and dividing by twelve. Estimated annual savings from a principal reduction can be found by multiplying the amount repaid by the annual rate. Daily savings can be approximated by multiplying the principal reduction by the annual rate and dividing by 365. These calculations will not always match the lender's statement exactly, but they provide a practical way to compare decisions and understand the cost of redrawing.

Daniel's final position is stronger because all parts of the strategy worked together. His balance is lower, his estimated interest expense has declined, his available credit has increased, his emergency reserve remains intact, and he has a lower internal borrowing limit for the next year. He has preserved access to capital without allowing that access to prevent debt reduction. This is the central purpose of a disciplined HELOC paydown-and-redraw system: to use flexibility when necessary while ensuring that the long-term direction remains toward lower debt, lower interest, and greater control of home equity.

Chapter 2

Establishing a Cash-Reserve Floor Before Paying Down the HELOC

Reducing a HELOC balance can lower interest expense, restore available credit, and move a homeowner closer to financial independence. However, the largest possible principal payment is not always the safest payment. Before directing surplus cash toward a HELOC, the homeowner must determine how much money needs to remain outside the credit line. This protected amount is the household's cash-reserve floor. It represents money that remains readily accessible without requiring lender approval, increasing debt, or placing additional pressure on the home.

A cash-reserve floor is especially important in a HELOC paydown-and-redraw strategy because available credit is not the same as available cash. Money held in a checking, savings, or money market account belongs to the homeowner and can generally be accessed according to the deposit account's terms. Unused HELOC capacity is money that the lender may allow the homeowner to borrow. It remains subject to the credit agreement, the remaining draw period, the condition of the account, and the lender's ability to restrict additional advances under certain circumstances. A homeowner who pays every available dollar into the HELOC may reduce interest temporarily but become dependent on the lender for the next financial emergency.

The purpose of the reserve floor is not to prevent aggressive debt reduction. Its purpose is to make debt reduction sustainable. If a homeowner applies too much cash to the HELOC and then has to redraw funds a few weeks later, the payment may produce only a small amount of interest savings. If the homeowner cannot redraw because the line has been frozen, reduced, or converted into repayment status, the household may have to rely on credit cards, personal loans, late payments, or the sale of assets. Preserving an appropriate amount of cash reduces the probability that an otherwise sound paydown plan will create a new financial problem.

The correct reserve is not determined by one universal number. A common starting point is to consider several months of essential household expenses, but the final amount should reflect the homeowner's complete financial situation. Two households with identical monthly expenses may require very different reserves. A household with two stable salaries, strong health insurance, a newer home, and no dependents may be able to operate with a smaller reserve than a household dependent on one self-employed income, supporting children, managing rental properties, and anticipating major repairs.

The first step in establishing the reserve floor is to calculate essential monthly expenses. Essential expenses are the obligations that must continue even if income declines. They ordinarily include mortgage payments, property taxes, homeowners insurance, utilities, basic food, transportation, health insurance, essential medical costs, minimum debt payments, and necessary childcare. Discretionary expenses such as entertainment, restaurant meals, optional travel, luxury purchases, and nonessential subscriptions should be separated from this calculation because they could be reduced during a financial interruption.

The homeowner should use realistic figures rather than optimistic estimates. If groceries normally cost $1,500 per month, the reserve calculation should not assume that the household can immediately reduce the expense to $600 unless such a change is practical. If utility bills fluctuate between seasons, an average based on the previous twelve months may be more reliable than the lowest recent bill. If annual insurance premiums or property taxes are not included in the mortgage payment, the monthly reserve calculation should include one-twelfth of those annual amounts.

After calculating essential monthly expenses, the homeowner selects a reserve period. A household with highly dependable income may begin with three months of essential expenses. A household with variable or commission-based income may prefer six months or more. A business owner whose revenue changes significantly throughout the year may need a reserve that covers a full low-income season. A real estate investor may need to protect both personal living reserves and separate property-level reserves for vacancies, repairs, insurance deductibles, taxes, and capital improvements.

Income concentration is one of the most important considerations. When a household depends almost entirely on one income source, the financial effect of losing or interrupting that source can be severe. A two-income household may still face risk if both earners work in the same business or industry because one economic event could affect both incomes simultaneously. The more concentrated the household's income, the larger its reserve may need to be before surplus cash is committed to HELOC principal.

Self-employed homeowners should examine the timing and reliability of business cash flow. Money that appears to be surplus in a personal account may be needed for quarterly taxes, payroll, inventory, insurance, licensing, advertising, or future operating expenses. A business owner should not use money reserved for known business obligations to reduce a personal HELOC merely because the funds are temporarily sitting in cash. The reserve analysis should distinguish true excess capital from money already assigned to future expenses.

Employment benefits also affect the reserve decision. A salaried employee may have paid leave, severance benefits, unemployment eligibility, disability coverage, or employer-sponsored health insurance. A self-employed person may have fewer protections and may need personal cash to replace those benefits during an interruption. The homeowner should evaluate how long income could realistically stop before alternative sources become available and how household costs might change if employment benefits were lost.

Property condition creates another layer of reserve needs. A homeowner with an aging roof, older air-conditioning systems, outdated plumbing, or evidence of structural problems should anticipate a higher probability of major expenses. Even when insurance may eventually cover a loss, deductibles and uncovered costs may need to be paid immediately. Insurance reimbursements can also take time. Maintaining property reserves outside the HELOC allows urgent repairs to proceed without assuming that the line will always remain accessible.

Insurance deductibles should be included directly in the reserve calculation. If the homeowners insurance policy has a $5,000 hurricane deductible and the health insurance plan has a $7,000 family deductible, the household could face significant out-of-pocket obligations. It may not be necessary to hold the full amount of every deductible in addition to several months of expenses, but the homeowner should account for the possibility that more than one financial event could occur during the same period. A reserve that covers only ordinary monthly bills may be inadequate when a major claim occurs.

The age and number of vehicles should also be considered. A household that depends on two older vehicles may face repair costs or the need for replacement transportation. If the vehicles are required for employment or business operations, a breakdown can reduce income as well as create an expense. A transportation reserve may therefore be part of the cash floor even when the household has access to a HELOC.

Family circumstances can raise or lower the required reserve. Households with young children, elderly dependents, ongoing medical needs, or tuition obligations may have limited ability to reduce expenses quickly. A single homeowner with flexible living costs may be able to adjust more easily. The reserve should reflect the household's actual responsibilities rather than an arbitrary percentage of income.

The remaining HELOC draw period must be considered because the ability to redraw will not continue indefinitely. A homeowner with many years remaining in the draw period may have more flexibility, although future access is still not guaranteed. A borrower with only several months remaining should be more cautious about placing cash into the line. Once the draw period ends, additional borrowing may no longer be available, and the required payment may increase as principal repayment begins. Cash that was paid into the HELOC shortly before the conversion may not be retrievable afterward.

A homeowner should also review the conditions under which the lender may suspend or reduce the line. The loan agreement may describe circumstances involving a decline in property value, a material change in the borrower's financial condition, payment problems, or other events. Understanding these provisions reinforces the difference between cash and borrowing capacity. The homeowner does not need to assume that the lender will restrict the line, but the financial plan should remain functional if access becomes limited.

Once the base reserve has been calculated, the homeowner should add money for known upcoming expenses. These may include property taxes, insurance premiums, tuition, medical procedures, vehicle repairs, home maintenance, travel required for family obligations, or business expenses. Known expenses should not be treated as unexpected emergencies. If a $6,000 insurance premium is due in three months, that money has already been assigned and should not ordinarily be counted as surplus available for permanent HELOC reduction.

The homeowner can organize cash into three conceptual layers. The first layer covers normal checking-account operations, including bills that will be paid during the current month. The second layer is the emergency reserve, which protects the household against income interruption and unexpected costs. The third layer contains true surplus cash that may be considered for HELOC paydown. Although these amounts may be held in one or more bank accounts, identifying their separate purposes prevents money needed for near-term obligations from being mistaken for excess capital.

Maintaining an operating buffer above the formal reserve floor can further reduce the likelihood of unnecessary redraws. If the calculated reserve is $30,000, the homeowner might maintain an additional $3,000 to $5,000 in checking for irregular monthly fluctuations. This buffer prevents ordinary timing differences from repeatedly pushing cash below the protected level. The homeowner can then direct amounts above the reserve and buffer toward the HELOC on a scheduled basis.

A staged paydown can be safer than one large transfer. Instead of applying the entire calculated surplus immediately, the homeowner may divide it into two or three payments over several months. This provides time to observe whether the reserve calculation was accurate. If no major expenses arise and income remains stable, the remaining planned payment can be made. If circumstances change, the homeowner retains the money without needing to redraw it.

For example, a household with $70,000 in cash may calculate a $40,000 emergency reserve, a $5,000 operating buffer, and $7,000 of known upcoming expenses. That leaves $18,000 that appears available for HELOC paydown. Rather than sending all $18,000 immediately, the homeowner could pay $10,000 now and schedule another review in 60 or 90 days. If the household's cash position remains stable, the remaining $8,000 can be paid later. The slightly slower approach sacrifices some potential interest savings but provides additional protection against an inaccurate estimate.

The reserve floor should not remain fixed forever. It should be reviewed when income, expenses, debt obligations, insurance coverage, family needs, or HELOC terms change. A homeowner who receives a significant salary increase and pays off a car loan may be able to reduce the number of months of expenses held in cash. A homeowner who leaves salaried employment to start a business may need to increase the reserve. A property owner who acquires another rental may need separate reserves for the new property before making additional HELOC payments.

The interest rate on the HELOC also influences the decision, but it should not override the need for liquidity. A high variable rate creates a strong mathematical incentive to reduce principal. However, an interest-saving strategy becomes less effective if the homeowner later borrows on a credit card at an even higher rate because too much cash was committed to the HELOC. The homeowner should compare the guaranteed savings from principal reduction with the financial risk created by holding less cash.

Opportunity cost should be evaluated carefully. Cash held in a savings account may earn a lower rate than the HELOC charges. If the HELOC costs 10 percent and savings earn 4 percent, paying down the HELOC may appear to produce a six-percentage-point advantage before considering taxes and other factors. That difference is meaningful, but it does not prove that every dollar of savings should be transferred. Part of the lower return on cash is the price paid for liquidity, certainty, and immediate access.

The homeowner can calculate a liquidity cost to understand this tradeoff. If $30,000 remains in savings earning 4 percent instead of being used to reduce a HELOC charging 10 percent, the gross rate difference is 6 percent. The approximate annual cost of maintaining that liquidity is $1,800. This does not automatically mean that keeping the cash is a mistake. It means the household is effectively accepting an estimated $1,800 difference in exchange for preserving $30,000 of dependable liquidity. The homeowner must determine whether that protection is worth the cost.

A reserve can also prevent forced sales of investments. Without adequate cash, a homeowner may have to sell stocks, retirement assets, or real estate during an unfavorable market. The tax consequences, penalties, lost future growth, or transaction costs could exceed the interest saved by making an oversized HELOC payment. A well-designed reserve allows long-term assets to remain invested while the household handles short-term disruptions.

Borrowers who want to accelerate paydown can use a surplus-cash rule. Under this method, the homeowner reviews cash at a predetermined interval, such as the end of every month. Any amount above the reserve floor, operating buffer, and known upcoming obligations is transferred to the HELOC. This creates consistent progress without relying on emotional decisions. The rule can be adjusted for irregular income by directing a percentage of bonuses, commissions, business distributions, or tax refunds toward principal.

A percentage system can protect both liquidity and progress. A self-employed homeowner might direct 50 percent of true monthly surplus toward the HELOC, retain 30 percent for future business or household needs, and allocate 20 percent to other financial goals. The exact percentages will differ among households. The important principle is that every dollar of surplus receives a purpose before it can be absorbed by discretionary spending.

The homeowner should establish a rule for replenishing the reserve after it is used. If an emergency reduces cash below the floor, additional HELOC paydown should ordinarily pause until the reserve is restored. Continuing aggressive principal payments while cash remains below the protected level can increase the risk of another redraw. Once the reserve returns to its target, the normal paydown schedule can resume.

The reserve floor should also be coordinated with the household's internal HELOC limit. The lender's approved limit may be much higher than the amount the homeowner is willing to owe. If a household has a $200,000 line but sets an internal maximum balance of $120,000, the homeowner should not raise that internal limit simply because cash reserves were underestimated. The proper response may be to pause paydown, reduce spending, rebuild cash, or create a specific short-term repayment plan for any necessary draw.

A disciplined reserve policy removes much of the uncertainty from HELOC management. The homeowner knows how much cash must remain untouched, which expenses are already funded, when additional payments can be made, and when paydown must pause. This structure reduces the temptation to alternate between excessively aggressive payments and unplanned borrowing. It transforms the HELOC from an emotional source of money into a controlled part of the household's financial system.

The central lesson is that preserving liquidity and reducing debt are not opposing goals. A properly calculated cash reserve supports long-term debt reduction because it lowers the probability that principal will need to be redrawn. The reserve protects the household while surplus cash reduces the balance. When both are managed together, the homeowner can lower interest, preserve future choices, and make progress without becoming dependent on continued access to borrowed capital.

Practical Math Example: Calculating a Safe Reserve and HELOC Paydown Amount

Consider a married couple, Anthony and Maria, who have a HELOC with a $200,000 credit limit and an outstanding balance of $145,000. Their variable interest rate is 10.20 percent, and four years remain in the draw period. They currently have $86,000 divided among checking, savings, and a money market account. They want to make a large principal payment because the HELOC's interest expense is placing pressure on their monthly cash flow.

Before transferring money, Anthony and Maria calculate their essential monthly expenses. Their first mortgage payment is $3,200. Property taxes and homeowners insurance not included in the mortgage average $900 per month when converted from annual amounts. Utilities, internet, and basic telephone service average $650. Groceries and necessary household supplies average $1,400. Transportation costs, including vehicle payments, insurance, fuel, and necessary maintenance, average $1,050. Health insurance and recurring medical expenses average $850. Minimum payments on other debts total $450. Their total essential monthly expenses are therefore $8,500.

Because Anthony owns a business and Maria earns a stable salary, they decide that five months of essential expenses is an appropriate starting point. They multiply $8,500 by five, producing a base emergency reserve of $42,500. This amount is intended to support the household if Anthony's business income falls substantially or if Maria temporarily loses her salary.

The couple then identifies known expenses that will occur during the next six months. Their annual property insurance premium requires an additional $4,000 payment that is not fully included in their current escrow arrangement. One vehicle needs approximately $2,000 of repairs, and they expect $3,500 in medical and dental expenses. Their known upcoming expenses total $9,500. Because these costs are reasonably predictable, Anthony and Maria do not classify the money as available surplus.

They also decide to maintain a $4,000 checking-account buffer above the emergency reserve. This amount will cover monthly fluctuations, irregular utility bills, school expenses, and timing differences between business income and household payments. Their total protected cash is calculated by adding the $42,500 emergency reserve, $9,500 of known expenses, and the $4,000 operating buffer. The result is $56,000.

Anthony and Maria subtract the $56,000 protected amount from their $86,000 of total cash. This leaves $30,000 that may be considered for HELOC paydown. However, they do not automatically transfer the entire $30,000. Because Anthony's business income varies, they choose to make an initial $20,000 payment and retain an additional $10,000 as a temporary secondary buffer. They plan to review that $10,000 after 90 days.

Before the payment, the simplified annual interest on their $145,000 HELOC balance is calculated by multiplying $145,000 by 10.20 percent. The result is $14,790 per year. Dividing that figure by twelve produces a simplified monthly interest estimate of $1,232.50. The lender's actual charge may differ because of daily balance calculations and the number of days in the billing cycle, but this estimate gives the couple a useful planning number.

After making the $20,000 principal payment, the HELOC balance falls from $145,000 to $125,000. Available credit increases from approximately $55,000 to approximately $75,000. The simplified annual interest at the new balance is calculated by multiplying $125,000 by 10.20 percent, producing $12,750. The simplified monthly interest estimate becomes $1,062.50.

The initial $20,000 payment creates estimated annual interest savings of $2,040. This can be calculated by subtracting the new annual interest estimate of $12,750 from the original estimate of $14,790. The same result can be found by multiplying the $20,000 principal reduction directly by the 10.20 percent annual rate. The estimated monthly savings are $170.

Anthony and Maria then calculate the approximate daily savings. They divide the 10.20 percent annual rate by 365, producing a daily periodic rate of approximately 0.027945 percent. Applying that daily rate to the $20,000 principal reduction produces estimated savings of approximately $5.59 per day. If the $20,000 remains undrawn for 90 days, the estimated savings are approximately $503.10.

After 90 days, the couple reviews its cash position. They began with $86,000 and paid $20,000 to the HELOC, leaving $66,000. During the 90-day period, they paid the planned $4,000 insurance cost, completed $2,000 in vehicle repairs, and paid $3,500 in medical and dental expenses. These expenses reduce cash by $9,500, bringing the balance to $56,500. They also generate $7,500 of new household surplus during the period, raising cash to $64,000.

Their protected base now consists of the $42,500 emergency reserve and the $4,000 operating buffer, for a total of $46,500. The previously known expenses have already been paid, so they no longer need to reserve another $9,500 for those obligations. Subtracting the $46,500 protected amount from their $64,000 cash balance leaves $17,500 of potential surplus.

The couple decides to retain $7,500 for upcoming business and household uncertainty and direct another $10,000 toward the HELOC. After this second payment, the balance falls from $125,000 to $115,000. The total principal reduction since the beginning of the plan is now $30,000. Their approximate available credit rises to $85,000.

At a $115,000 balance and a 10.20 percent annual rate, the simplified annual interest estimate is $11,730. Dividing by twelve produces an estimated monthly interest charge of $977.50. Compared with the original monthly estimate of $1,232.50, Anthony and Maria are now saving approximately $255 per month. The estimated annual difference is $3,060.

Although the lender shows approximately $85,000 of available credit, the couple does not treat that amount as an emergency fund. Their emergency reserve remains in cash. They also establish an internal HELOC balance limit of $125,000, meaning they will not permit the balance to exceed that amount except in an extreme situation. With a current balance of $115,000, they have only $10,000 of self-approved redraw capacity even though the lender may allow substantially more.

Two months later, Anthony's business experiences a delayed customer payment. He needs $6,000 to cover an essential business expense that cannot be postponed. He expects the customer's $18,000 payment within 45 days, but the money has not yet been received. Anthony and Maria consider using cash, but doing so would bring their household accounts too close to the reserve floor. They decide to draw $6,000 from the HELOC and establish a repayment plan tied to the expected customer payment.

The $6,000 draw raises the HELOC balance from $115,000 to $121,000. The balance remains below their $125,000 internal limit. At 10.20 percent, the simplified annual interest associated with the $6,000 draw is $612. If the draw remains outstanding for 45 days, the simplified cost can be estimated by multiplying $6,000 by 10.20 percent and then multiplying the result by 45 divided by 365. The estimated interest cost for the 45-day period is approximately $75.45.

When the $18,000 customer payment arrives, Anthony sets aside $4,500 for taxes and $3,500 for continuing business expenses. This leaves $10,000. He uses $6,000 to repay the HELOC draw and applies another $2,000 as permanent principal reduction. The remaining $2,000 stays in the business account. After the $8,000 payment is applied, the HELOC balance falls from $121,000 to $113,000.

At the new $113,000 balance, simplified annual interest is approximately $11,526, and simplified monthly interest is approximately $960.50. Compared with the original $145,000 balance, the couple has achieved a net principal reduction of $32,000. Multiplying $32,000 by 10.20 percent produces estimated annual interest savings of $3,264, or approximately $272 per month.

The couple then creates a goal of reducing the HELOC balance to $105,000 during the next eight months. The difference between the current $113,000 balance and the $105,000 target is $8,000. Dividing $8,000 by eight months produces a permanent principal target of $1,000 per month. This amount must be paid in addition to the interest that accrues.

At the current balance, the simplified monthly interest estimate is $960.50. To reduce principal by approximately $1,000 during the next month, Anthony and Maria would need to make a total payment of approximately $1,960.50, assuming no new draws, fees, or interest-rate changes. As the principal balance declines, the interest portion should also decline if the rate remains constant, allowing slightly more of a consistent total payment to reach principal.

Suppose they pay $2,000 per month for the next eight months and the rate remains at 10.20 percent. A precise calculation would account for daily interest and the declining balance, but a simplified estimate can still show the general result. If the average monthly interest during this period is approximately $930, about $1,070 of each $2,000 payment would reduce principal. Over eight months, the estimated principal reduction would be approximately $8,560.

Under this simplified projection, the HELOC balance would fall from $113,000 to approximately $104,440. This would place the couple about $560 below its $105,000 target. At a $104,440 balance and a 10.20 percent annual rate, the simplified monthly interest would be approximately $887.74. Compared with the original estimate of $1,232.50, the monthly interest difference would be approximately $344.76.

The couple's result was not produced by sending all $86,000 of their cash to the HELOC. If they had done so, the balance would have fallen dramatically, but they would have had no dependable cash for household expenses, insurance, vehicle repairs, medical costs, or business interruptions. They might have been forced to redraw significant amounts, and any restriction on the line could have created a serious liquidity crisis.

Instead, Anthony and Maria separated protected cash from true surplus. They calculated essential expenses, selected an appropriate number of reserve months, funded known obligations, maintained an operating buffer, and used staged principal payments. When they later needed a temporary business draw, they remained within their internal limit and repaid the draw from an identified revenue source. Their reserve allowed them to make long-term progress without placing every financial need under the lender's control.

This example demonstrates that the safest HELOC payment is not necessarily the largest amount that can be transferred today. It is the largest amount that can remain paid down without weakening the household's ability to manage predictable bills and unexpected events. Anthony and Maria lowered their balance, reduced estimated interest, preserved their emergency cash, and maintained controlled access to capital. Their reserve floor did not prevent debt reduction; it made sustained debt reduction possible.

Chapter 3

Using Payment Timing to Reduce the HELOC's Average Daily Balance

The amount of principal paid toward a HELOC is important, but the timing of that payment can also affect the total interest charged. Many HELOCs calculate interest using the outstanding balance for each day of the billing cycle. Under this structure, a principal payment made near the beginning of the cycle can reduce the balance subject to interest for more days than the same payment made near the end. A homeowner who understands this relationship can use income timing, scheduled expenses, and planned redraws more efficiently.

The mathematical foundation of this strategy is the daily periodic rate. A lender generally begins with the HELOC's annual percentage rate and divides it by 365 days, although the exact calculation method should be confirmed in the loan agreement. The resulting daily rate is applied to the principal balance for each day. The lender then adds the daily interest amounts to determine the interest charged for the billing period. If the balance changes during the month because of payments or draws, each daily balance contributes differently to the final charge.

Suppose a homeowner owes $100,000 on a HELOC with a 10 percent annual rate. A simplified daily periodic rate can be calculated by dividing 10 percent by 365. The result is approximately 0.027397 percent per day. When applied to a $100,000 balance, the approximate daily interest is $27.40. If the homeowner reduces the balance by $20,000, the daily interest associated with that portion is eliminated while the payment remains applied. At a 10 percent annual rate, the approximate daily savings on the $20,000 principal reduction are $5.48.

If the $20,000 payment is made on the first day of a 30-day billing cycle and remains in the HELOC for the entire cycle, the simplified interest savings are approximately $164.40. If the same payment is made on day 20, it reduces the balance for only about ten days, creating simplified savings of approximately $54.80. The homeowner pays the same $20,000 in both situations, but the earlier payment creates approximately $109.60 more savings during that billing cycle because the balance remains lower for an additional 20 days.

This does not mean a homeowner should make a payment before having sufficient money available. The timing strategy should be used only after preserving the cash-reserve floor, funding known expenses, and confirming that the money represents true surplus or a carefully planned temporary paydown. Sending money to the HELOC early and then using a high-cost credit card to cover ordinary bills would defeat the purpose. Payment timing improves an already sound cash-management plan; it cannot correct an inadequate reserve or a recurring budget deficit.

A homeowner should begin by reviewing the HELOC statement and loan agreement. The borrower needs to determine the billing-cycle dates, payment due date, interest calculation method, payment-processing rules, and availability of repaid principal. The due date identifies when the required payment must be received, but it does not necessarily identify the most effective day for making an extra principal payment. A borrower who waits until the due date may keep the account current while missing several weeks of potential balance reduction.

The distinction between the statement date and payment due date is particularly important. The statement date usually marks the end of one billing cycle and summarizes the activity that occurred during that period. The due date may be several weeks later. If the borrower receives income shortly after the statement is issued and waits until the due date to make a principal payment, the higher balance may continue generating interest during much of the next cycle. An earlier payment could reduce that interest, provided the household retains enough liquidity for expenses.

Homeowners who receive regular paychecks can coordinate extra principal payments with each payday. Instead of accumulating surplus cash throughout the month and sending one payment at the end, the borrower may send smaller payments whenever income is received. If a household can devote $2,000 per month to HELOC principal, it might pay $1,000 after the first paycheck and $1,000 after the second paycheck. This approach causes part of the monthly principal reduction to occur earlier and may lower the average daily balance.

A household paid twice per month should not automatically transfer all remaining income to the HELOC after each paycheck. The borrower should first account for bills due before the next paycheck, maintain the established checking buffer, and protect the emergency reserve. Only the amount above these needs should be considered for early payment. An automated or percentage-based system can make this process more consistent, but automation should never remove the need to monitor cash flow.

Weekly income can create even more opportunities for incremental reduction. A business owner, freelancer, or commission-based worker may receive deposits at irregular intervals. Each time income arrives, the borrower can separate taxes, business expenses, personal expenses, reserve contributions, and true surplus. The surplus portion can then be applied to the HELOC promptly rather than remaining idle until the end of the month. The savings from each payment may appear small, but repeated reductions can create a meaningful cumulative effect.

The average daily balance helps explain why repeated early payments can work. If a balance remains at $100,000 for the entire month, its average daily balance is $100,000. If a $10,000 payment reduces the balance to $90,000 halfway through a 30-day month, the average daily balance is approximately $95,000. The balance was $100,000 for 15 days and $90,000 for 15 days, so the weighted average equals $95,000. Interest for the cycle is therefore closer to the amount generated by a $95,000 balance than by either the opening or closing balance alone.

A closing balance does not tell the complete story. Two borrowers can end the month owing the same amount but pay different interest because their balances followed different paths. One borrower may reduce the balance early and keep it lower throughout the cycle. Another may carry a high balance for most of the month and make a large payment immediately before the statement closes. Both statements may show the same ending balance, yet the first borrower may owe less interest because the average daily balance was lower.

The timing of redraws matters for the same reason. If a homeowner expects to pay a $12,000 expense near the end of the month, there may be no reason to draw the money several weeks in advance unless the vendor requires an earlier payment or there is a legitimate concern about access to the line. Drawing the money early increases the number of days on which interest accrues. Waiting until the funds are actually needed can reduce interest, assuming the borrower has confirmed that the line is open, the draw can be processed on time, and no transaction delays will interfere with the payment.

Suppose a $12,000 draw carries a 10 percent annual rate. The approximate daily interest on that amount is $3.29. Drawing the money 20 days before it is needed creates approximately $65.80 of additional interest compared with drawing it on the day of use. The amount may not appear large in isolation, but unnecessary early draws repeated throughout the year can add hundreds or thousands of dollars to borrowing costs.

Payment-processing time must be incorporated into the strategy. A payment initiated on a particular date may not be credited to the account until the next business day or later. Transfers from an outside bank may take several days. Weekend and holiday schedules may also delay processing. The homeowner should verify when the lender considers a payment effective rather than assuming that the date on which the transfer is requested is the date on which interest stops accruing on that principal.

The same caution applies to redraws. A homeowner should not postpone a necessary draw until the last possible moment if the payment must be available by a strict deadline. An electronic transfer, check, or bank-to-bank movement may require processing time. The objective is to avoid borrowing significantly earlier than necessary while still allowing enough time for the transaction to clear.

A payment-timing strategy can be organized around a monthly cash-flow calendar. The homeowner records expected income dates, recurring bill dates, irregular expenses, the HELOC statement date, and the payment due date. This calendar reveals which cash is temporarily available and which money has already been assigned to upcoming obligations. Surplus amounts can be transferred earlier, while anticipated draws can be scheduled closer to the date on which the funds will be used.

For example, a homeowner may receive $12,000 in household income on the first day of the month and another $8,000 on the fifteenth. Essential expenses of $13,000 may be spread throughout the month. After reserving the required amount for bills and maintaining the checking buffer, the household may determine that $3,000 can be paid toward the HELOC on day one and another $2,000 on day fifteen. Sending the full $5,000 at the end of the month would produce the same closing principal balance, but it would not produce the same average daily balance.

Irregular income requires a more conservative method. A business owner may receive $30,000 early in one month and only $5,000 the next month. Applying the entire first deposit to the HELOC could create strong short-term interest savings but force a large redraw during the weaker month. A better approach may be to retain the amount required for taxes, operating costs, personal expenses, and the cash-reserve floor while applying only the verified surplus. The business owner can still benefit from early payment without placing essential liquidity at risk.

Tax money deserves particular protection. Self-employed homeowners may receive gross deposits that appear large but contain money owed for federal, state, payroll, or sales taxes. Sending tax reserves to the HELOC may reduce interest temporarily, but it converts a known future obligation into dependence on available credit. If the borrower uses a temporary paydown approach with tax funds, the strategy should be carefully documented, the payment date should be known, and enough time should remain to redraw and transfer the money. A more conservative homeowner may decide that tax funds should never be placed into the HELOC.

Escrowed or restricted business money should also be excluded. Customer deposits, payroll funds, tenant security deposits, and money held for a specific project may not represent free cash. Using such money to reduce personal debt, even temporarily, can create legal, accounting, operational, or contractual problems. The HELOC strategy should use only money that the homeowner is authorized to control and that is not restricted for another purpose.

A temporary paydown should always have an exit date. If a homeowner applies $15,000 that will be needed for an insurance premium in 60 days, the borrower should record the expected redraw date, the amount required, and the payment deadline. During the 60-day period, the lower HELOC balance may reduce interest. As the deadline approaches, the borrower confirms that the credit remains available and initiates the draw early enough for the funds to clear. Without this documentation, temporarily deposited money may be mistaken for permanent principal reduction and spent elsewhere.

The borrower should also calculate whether the temporary paydown creates enough benefit to justify the operational risk. At a 10 percent annual rate, a $15,000 temporary payment held for 60 days saves approximately $246.58 before considering any transaction fees or other costs. If the lender charges a draw fee, transfer fee, or minimum finance charge, the net benefit will be smaller. If there is a meaningful possibility that the line could be frozen, risking access to a $15,000 insurance payment for a few hundred dollars of savings may not be appropriate.

Interest-rate changes can alter the savings produced by payment timing. Because many HELOC rates are variable, the annual rate may rise or fall during the plan. When the rate rises, each dollar of early principal reduction creates greater interest savings, but each redraw also becomes more expensive. The homeowner should update the daily and monthly calculations whenever the rate changes rather than relying on figures developed when the line carried a lower rate.

The borrower can measure payment-timing performance by comparing the opening balance, average daily balance, and closing balance. The opening balance shows where the cycle began, the closing balance shows where it ended, and the average daily balance indicates how much principal was generating interest throughout the cycle. A declining closing balance is important, but a consistently lower average daily balance demonstrates that payments are being applied early enough to reduce interest throughout the month.

A homeowner should avoid making excessive transactions solely to capture very small savings. Sending numerous daily payments can complicate recordkeeping, create payment-processing errors, or make it harder to maintain a clear budget. A simple system based on paydays or scheduled monthly review dates may capture most of the potential benefit without unnecessary complexity. Consistency is more valuable than creating a system that is mathematically precise but difficult to maintain.

Extra payments should be verified after processing. The homeowner should confirm that the balance declined, the payment was applied correctly, and the available credit increased as expected. If a payment is returned because of insufficient funds or an account error, the borrower could face fees and lose anticipated interest savings. Keeping a reasonable checking buffer protects against such mistakes.

Payment timing must remain subordinate to the long-term goal of permanent balance reduction. A borrower who deposits income into the HELOC at the beginning of every month but redraws the same amount for discretionary spending before the month ends may create only minor interest savings. The account may remain active while the year-end balance stays unchanged. A successful system uses early payments to support a declining balance, not to disguise the fact that spending continues to consume every dollar of income.

The homeowner can create separate targets for timing and principal reduction. The timing target might require surplus payments to be made within two business days of receiving income. The principal target might require the ending balance to decline by at least $1,000 per month after all redraws. The first rule helps reduce the average daily balance, while the second ensures that the strategy produces permanent progress.

A disciplined borrower also evaluates the reason for every redraw. Necessary expenses with a defined repayment source may fit the plan, while routine consumption should ordinarily be funded through the household budget. Delaying a legitimate draw until the funds are needed reduces interest, but refusing to address a persistent budget deficit merely postpones the underlying problem. The homeowner must maintain both mathematical control and spending discipline.

The greatest value of payment timing comes from combining several small advantages. Early principal payments reduce the number of days on which interest accrues. Delayed draws prevent interest from beginning before borrowed funds are needed. Multiple payments aligned with income can lower the average daily balance. A protected reserve prevents the homeowner from reversing those payments prematurely. Over many months, these practices can support meaningful interest savings and faster balance reduction.

The central principle is straightforward: interest depends not only on how much is borrowed, but also on how long that amount remains outstanding. A homeowner cannot always control the HELOC's variable rate, but the homeowner can influence the daily balance. By paying true surplus earlier, drawing funds only when needed, preserving adequate liquidity, and monitoring actual account activity, the borrower can make the revolving structure work more efficiently.

Practical Math Example: Comparing Early Payments, Late Payments, and Planned Redraws

Consider a homeowner named Rebecca who has a HELOC balance of $160,000 and an annual variable rate of 10.50 percent. Her billing cycle contains 30 days. She has already established a sufficient emergency reserve, funded her known expenses, and determined that she can permanently apply $12,000 of surplus income to the HELOC during the current month. She wants to understand how payment timing will affect the interest charged.

Rebecca first calculates the approximate daily periodic rate by dividing 10.50 percent by 365. The result is approximately 0.028767 percent per day. The approximate daily interest on the original $160,000 balance is found by multiplying $160,000 by 0.105 and dividing by 365. This produces approximately $46.03 of interest per day.

If Rebecca makes no principal payment until the end of the 30-day billing cycle, the $160,000 balance remains outstanding for all 30 days. Multiplying the approximate daily interest of $46.03 by 30 produces estimated cycle interest of $1,380.90. If she then makes the $12,000 payment on the final day, her closing balance falls to $148,000, but the payment has produced almost no interest savings during the completed cycle because the higher balance remained outstanding for nearly the entire period.

Rebecca compares that result with making the full $12,000 payment on the first day. Her balance would immediately fall from $160,000 to $148,000. The approximate daily interest on $148,000 at 10.50 percent is calculated by multiplying $148,000 by 0.105 and dividing by 365. The result is approximately $42.58 per day. Multiplying $42.58 by 30 days produces estimated cycle interest of approximately $1,277.40.

The difference between the late-payment scenario and the early-payment scenario is approximately $103.50 for the 30-day cycle. Rebecca ends the month with the same $148,000 principal balance in both scenarios, but making the payment on day one reduces the amount generating interest throughout the month. This comparison demonstrates why the closing balance alone does not reveal the full cost of carrying the HELOC.

Rebecca is paid twice during the month and may not have the full $12,000 available on the first day. She therefore considers a third scenario. She can pay $6,000 on day one and another $6,000 on day sixteen. Under this plan, the balance would be $154,000 for the first 15 days and $148,000 for the remaining 15 days.

The approximate daily interest on a $154,000 balance at 10.50 percent is $44.30. Multiplying $44.30 by 15 days produces approximately $664.50 of interest for the first half of the cycle. The approximate daily interest on the $148,000 balance is $42.58. Multiplying $42.58 by 15 days produces approximately $638.70 for the second half. Total estimated interest for the cycle is therefore approximately $1,303.20.

The twice-monthly payment method produces estimated interest of $1,303.20, compared with approximately $1,380.90 when the full payment is delayed until the end. Rebecca saves approximately $77.70 during the cycle by paying according to her income dates. The twice-monthly method costs approximately $25.80 more than paying the full $12,000 on day one, but it reflects the actual timing of her available income and does not require her to weaken her cash reserve.

Rebecca calculates the average daily balance for each scenario. When the $12,000 payment is delayed until the end of the cycle, the average daily balance is approximately $160,000. When the full payment is made on day one, the average daily balance is $148,000. When $6,000 is paid on day one and another $6,000 is paid halfway through the cycle, the average daily balance is approximately $151,000. This is calculated by multiplying $154,000 by 15 days, multiplying $148,000 by 15 days, adding the results, and dividing by 30.

The average daily balance explains the interest differences. The end-of-cycle payment leaves the highest average balance. The full day-one payment creates the lowest average balance. The twice-monthly method falls between the two. Rebecca chooses the twice-monthly method because it matches her pay schedule and preserves sufficient operating cash while still capturing most of the available timing benefit.

During the next billing cycle, Rebecca expects to pay $9,000 for a home improvement on day 25. The contractor does not require a deposit, and payment will be due only after the work is completed. Rebecca could draw the $9,000 from the HELOC on day one, but doing so would cause interest to accrue for 24 days before the money is needed.

At an annual rate of 10.50 percent, the approximate daily interest on a $9,000 draw is calculated by multiplying $9,000 by 0.105 and dividing by 365. The result is approximately $2.59 per day. Drawing the money 24 days early would create approximately $62.16 of additional interest. Rebecca therefore schedules the draw close to day 25 while allowing enough processing time for the funds to reach her bank account.

Rebecca confirms that electronic draws normally require two business days. Because day 25 falls on a Wednesday, she initiates the draw on

Monday. The money reaches her bank account in time to pay the contractor. Instead of paying interest for approximately 24 days before the expense, she pays interest for only the short processing period and the time after the draw remains outstanding.

Before borrowing, Rebecca creates a repayment plan. She expects a $5,000 work bonus in 30 days and can contribute another $1,000 from each of her next four paychecks. The bonus and paycheck allocations will provide the full $9,000 needed to repay the draw. She does not include the anticipated bonus in her emergency reserve because it has not yet been received.

After the $9,000 draw, Rebecca's balance rises from $148,000 to $157,000. At 10.50 percent, the simplified monthly interest associated with the $9,000 draw is approximately $78.75. This is calculated by multiplying $9,000 by 10.50 percent and dividing by twelve. If the balance remains outstanding for only 30 days, the actual cost should be close to this simplified estimate, depending on the lender's daily calculation and the number of days in the cycle.

Rebecca receives her first paycheck two weeks after the draw and applies $1,000 toward the borrowed amount. The balance falls from $157,000 to $156,000. Two weeks later, she receives the $5,000 bonus and her next paycheck. She applies the full $5,000 bonus and another $1,000 from the paycheck, reducing the balance from $156,000 to $150,000. The remaining portion of the home-improvement draw is now $2,000.

Rebecca applies $1,000 from each of the next two paychecks. After the final payment, the balance returns to $148,000. The entire $9,000 home-improvement draw has been repaid. Because she paid portions of the draw before the end of the repayment period, the average balance was lower than it would have been if she had waited and made one $9,000 payment at the end.

Rebecca then makes an additional permanent principal payment of $2,000 from income above her reserve and scheduled obligations. Her balance falls from $148,000 to $146,000. She has paid for the home improvement, repaid the related draw, and continued reducing the long-term HELOC balance.

At the original $160,000 balance and a 10.50 percent rate, simplified annual interest would be $16,800. At the new $146,000 balance, simplified annual interest is $15,330. The $14,000 permanent principal reduction creates estimated annual savings of $1,470, or approximately $122.50 per month, as long as the rate and balance remain unchanged.

Rebecca wants to understand the cumulative value of making her regular payments earlier. She expects to reduce principal by $2,000 per month for the next twelve months. If she waits until the end of every month, each payment will affect the following month but provide little benefit during the current month. If she instead pays $1,000 on day one and $1,000 on day sixteen, an average of approximately $1,500 of that month's planned reduction will be reflected in the average daily balance during the cycle.

At a 10.50 percent annual rate, reducing the average daily balance by approximately $1,500 during one month saves about $13.13 for that cycle. The calculation is simplified by multiplying $1,500 by 10.50 percent and dividing by twelve. Repeating the timing strategy each month may add roughly $157.50 of first-year savings beyond the savings produced by the declining principal itself. The precise result will depend on exact payment dates, billing-cycle lengths, rate changes, and the progressively lower balance.

The timing benefit is smaller than the savings created by permanent principal reduction, but it still contributes to the overall strategy. Rebecca does not allow the pursuit of an additional $10 or $15 of monthly savings to place her checking account at risk. She keeps her reserve intact and schedules payments only after confirming that upcoming bills are funded.

Rebecca also avoids moving money back and forth unnecessarily. She does not send funds to the HELOC if she knows they will be needed again within several days. The interest savings from such a short temporary payment could be insignificant, while processing delays and bookkeeping complexity could create problems. She focuses on payments that will remain applied long enough to produce a meaningful benefit.

At the end of each billing cycle, Rebecca records the opening balance, payments, draws, interest charged, closing balance, and average daily balance shown by the lender when available. She compares the actual interest with her estimate. Small differences are expected because her simplified calculations do not account for every processing date, rate adjustment, or day-count convention. The purpose of the calculations is to guide decisions and reveal the approximate cost of different timing choices.

Rebecca's example shows that an effective HELOC strategy manages both sides of the account. She makes principal payments as early as her cash flow safely permits, and she delays draws until the borrowed money is genuinely needed. When she does redraw, she identifies the repayment sources in advance and returns the balance to its previous level before making additional permanent progress.

The practical result is a lower average daily balance, reduced interest expense, and a declining long-term principal balance. Payment timing does not replace the need to control spending or maintain a cash reserve, but it improves the efficiency of a disciplined plan. By understanding that each dollar generates interest for every day it remains outstanding, a homeowner can make better decisions about when to pay, when to draw, and how long any redrawn amount should remain on the HELOC.

Chapter 4

Creating Redraw Rules and Assigning a Repayment Source

A successful HELOC paydown strategy is determined not only by how much principal the homeowner repays, but also by what happens after that principal becomes available to borrow again. Every principal payment may restore part of the line's available credit during the draw period. If the restored availability is used casually, the balance can return to its former level or rise even higher. The homeowner may appear to be making progress because large payments are regularly deposited into the line, yet the long-term balance may remain unchanged. Creating written redraw rules prevents restored credit from turning into an invitation to spend.

A redraw rule establishes the circumstances under which money may be borrowed again after principal has been repaid. The rule should be created before the need or opportunity arises. Decisions made during an emergency, a business expansion, a home renovation, or an emotionally appealing purchase are often influenced by urgency and optimism. A predetermined standard gives the homeowner a consistent method for evaluating the draw when emotions, sales pressure, or financial stress might otherwise weaken judgment.

The first redraw rule should define which purposes qualify for HELOC use. Appropriate categories might include critical home repairs, major uninsured medical expenses, carefully evaluated business costs, temporary income interruptions, or property improvements supported by a realistic budget. The homeowner may also reserve part of the line for an investment opportunity, but the expected return should be analyzed conservatively.

Labeling an expense as an investment does not eliminate the interest expense, variable-rate risk, repayment obligation, or possibility of loss.

The second rule should identify purposes that do not qualify. Ordinary groceries, restaurant meals, entertainment, recurring utilities, clothing, vacations, subscriptions, holiday spending, and routine household costs should generally be funded through monthly income. If these expenses repeatedly require HELOC draws, the household may be operating with a structural cash-flow deficit. Borrowing against the home can temporarily conceal the deficit, but it does not solve it. The balance will continue growing until spending is reduced, income is increased, or another permanent adjustment is made.

Some expenses fall between clearly necessary and clearly discretionary categories. A kitchen renovation may correct serious damage, improve the home's functionality, or simply satisfy a preference for a newer design. A vehicle purchase may be necessary for employment, but the selected vehicle may cost substantially more than a dependable alternative. A business draw may preserve operations or fund an uncertain expansion. These situations require the homeowner to separate the essential portion of the expense from the optional portion.

The third rule should establish the maximum draw amount. The lender's available credit should never automatically become the homeowner's approved spending amount. If the HELOC has $100,000 of available credit, the borrower may still decide that no individual draw can exceed $15,000 without a complete review. A lower internal limit reduces the risk that one decision will reverse years of principal reduction.

The maximum draw should be based on repayment capacity rather than available credit. A household that can reliably direct $1,000 per month toward principal should recognize that a $12,000 draw requires approximately one year to repay before considering interest and other activity. A $36,000 draw could require three years at the same principal rate. The borrower should calculate how long the new debt will remain outstanding and determine whether that timeline is consistent with the remaining draw period and long-term balance targets.

The fourth redraw rule should require a specific repayment source. The homeowner should identify where the money will come from before the draw occurs. A repayment source may be monthly surplus income, a signed business receivable, a scheduled bonus, rental income, an insurance reimbursement, the sale of an asset, or another reasonably dependable source. The repayment source should be documented by more than a general expectation that income will improve.

A future salary is not automatically a repayment plan. If all regular salary is already assigned to household expenses, minimum debt payments, savings, and other obligations, there may be no surplus available to repay the new draw. The homeowner must calculate the amount of income remaining after essential expenses. Only that actual surplus can support the repayment schedule unless another source is clearly identified.

A business receivable may be a reasonable repayment source, but it should still be evaluated cautiously. A signed contract is stronger than a verbal promise, and a completed invoice owed by an established customer may be stronger than projected revenue from a new product. Even documented payments can be delayed or disputed. A business owner using a receivable as the repayment source should preserve enough flexibility to continue making payments if the customer pays later than expected.

Expected tax refunds should also be treated conservatively. The amount may be smaller than anticipated, processing may be delayed, or the refund may be applied to another obligation. If a tax refund is used as a repayment source, the homeowner should avoid borrowing the full expected amount. A margin of safety allows for changes between the estimate and the amount actually received.

The fifth rule should establish a repayment deadline. A redraw without a deadline can quietly become permanent debt. If a homeowner borrows $10,000 and simply plans to pay extra whenever possible, competing expenses may continually postpone repayment. A defined deadline creates a measurable obligation. The deadline might be three months for a draw supported by an upcoming bonus, twelve months for a home repair, or another period justified by the homeowner's cash flow.

The repayment deadline should be converted into a monthly principal target. If a $12,000 draw must be repaid within twelve months, the borrower needs to reduce principal by an average of $1,000 per month in addition to paying the interest generated by the line. If the required HELOC payment covers only interest, making a total payment of $1,000 will not reduce the draw by the full amount. The homeowner must distinguish the interest portion from the additional principal needed to meet the deadline.

The sixth rule should establish a stress-tested payment. Because many HELOCs carry variable rates, the borrower should calculate whether the redraw remains manageable if the interest rate rises. A draw that appears affordable at 8 percent may create significantly more interest at 11 percent or 12 percent. The principal-repayment target may remain the same, but the total monthly payment needed to cover both principal and interest will increase.

The homeowner should also consider the possibility that the planned repayment source will arrive late. If a $15,000 draw is expected to be repaid by a business receivable in 60 days, the borrower should calculate what will happen if the payment takes 120 days. The household should be capable of covering the additional interest and minimum payments during the delay without using another draw. A plan that works only when every event occurs on the earliest possible date is too fragile.

The seventh rule should protect the cash-reserve floor. The homeowner should not use an approved redraw as a reason to eliminate cash reserves. If the HELOC is used for an emergency, the reserve may also be affected by the same event. The plan should explain whether future surplus will first repay the draw, replenish the reserve, or divide money between both objectives. The proper order depends on the size of the remaining cash reserve, the HELOC rate, and the household's exposure to further emergencies.

The eighth rule should preserve an internal maximum HELOC balance. This limit is the highest balance the homeowner is willing to carry regardless of the amount approved by the lender. Suppose a lender provides a $250,000 limit, but the homeowner establishes an internal ceiling of $140,000. If the current balance is $132,000, the household has only $8,000 of self-approved capacity. The fact that the lender shows $118,000 of unused credit does not change the homeowner's personal limit.

An internal ceiling should generally move downward over time. If the homeowner's objective is to reduce debt while retaining access to capital, the maximum acceptable balance should not remain fixed forever. The household might reduce its internal ceiling from $140,000 to $125,000 after one year and to $110,000 after another. This approach permits limited redraws but prevents the account from returning to its original high balance.

The ninth rule should prohibit overlapping redraws unless the combined obligations have been reviewed. A homeowner may borrow $8,000 for a roof repair, then $5,000 for a business expense, and later $4,000 for medical costs. Each draw may appear manageable separately, but the combined $17,000 balance increase can overwhelm the repayment plan. Before approving a new draw, the borrower should calculate the total amount of existing redraws, remaining repayment periods, and combined monthly principal targets.

Separate tracking is essential because the HELOC statement will usually combine all draws into one balance. The lender may not distinguish the roof repair from the business expense or the medical bill. The homeowner should maintain a record of each draw's date, amount, purpose, rate at the time of borrowing, repayment source, scheduled payment, remaining balance, and deadline. This internal accounting makes it possible to determine whether each borrowing decision is performing as planned.

A written redraw register can prevent repaid money from being misallocated. If the homeowner sends an additional $3,000 to the HELOC, the register can show whether that payment repaid a specific draw or represented permanent principal reduction. Without this distinction, the borrower may believe an old draw has been eliminated when the total balance has merely been moved by unrelated activity.

The tenth rule should require a waiting period for nonemergency draws. A delay of 24 hours, 72 hours, or one week gives the homeowner time to compare alternatives, obtain additional estimates, and reconsider the expense. Immediate action may be necessary for a broken air-conditioning system, urgent medical treatment, or property damage. It is rarely necessary for a cosmetic renovation, discretionary purchase, or speculative investment.

During the waiting period, the borrower should compare other funding sources. Cash above the reserve floor, a low-rate promotional offer, business financing, insurance proceeds, vendor financing, or a scheduled payment plan may cost less or place the home at less risk. The HELOC may still be the preferred option, but the decision should result from comparison rather than convenience.

The borrower should also evaluate whether the expense can be reduced, delayed, or completed in stages. A $30,000 project might contain $18,000 of necessary work and $12,000 of optional upgrades. Borrowing only for the necessary portion lowers interest and shortens the repayment period. Staging the optional work allows future cash flow to fund improvements without increasing the HELOC balance.

Every redraw should pass a benefit-versus-cost test. The expected benefit should be compared with interest, fees, variable-rate exposure, repayment pressure, and the risk created by securing the borrowing with the home. If a $20,000 business investment is expected to produce only $1,000 of additional annual profit while the HELOC charges 10 percent, the expected return may not cover the approximate $2,000 of first-year interest. The homeowner would be accepting substantial risk for a negative projected spread.

Expected returns should be calculated conservatively. Business expansions and property improvements often cost more and take longer than originally planned. A homeowner should create a base estimate, a conservative estimate, and a downside estimate. If the draw is manageable only under the most optimistic forecast, it should be reconsidered. The borrower should be able to repay the debt even if the expected benefit is delayed or reduced.

Home improvements require a similar analysis. A project costing $40,000 does not necessarily increase the property's market value by $40,000. Some improvements primarily increase comfort or personal enjoyment. That may still be a valid use of money, but the borrower should not justify the entire draw as an investment unless market evidence supports the expected increase in value. The repayment plan must come from household cash flow rather than depending entirely on a future home sale.

The homeowner should create an approval question that summarizes the rules. Before drawing, the borrower asks whether the expense is approved, whether the amount is limited to what is necessary, whether a repayment source exists, whether a deadline has been established, whether the monthly payment is affordable, whether the draw stays below the internal ceiling, and whether the reserve remains protected. If the transaction fails any essential part of the test, it should be delayed, reduced, or rejected.

Households with more than one decision-maker should agree on the redraw rules together. One spouse should not make a major draw without the other understanding the purpose, amount, and repayment plan. Shared rules reduce conflict and prevent different interpretations of available credit. The household can establish a dollar threshold above which both parties must approve the transaction.

The rules should also address access methods. Convenience checks, debit cards, and instant transfers can make HELOC borrowing feel similar to spending from a checking account. The homeowner may choose to disable unnecessary access methods, store checks securely, or require a deliberate transfer process. Adding a small amount of friction can prevent impulsive draws without interfering with legitimate use.

A redraw plan should be reviewed after the transaction occurs. The homeowner should confirm the amount borrowed, effective interest rate, transaction date, fees, new total balance, and available credit. If the draw is larger than expected or the rate has changed, the repayment calculation must be updated. The borrower should not wait until the next annual review to discover that the plan no longer works.

Monthly progress should be measured against the scheduled balance. If a $12,000 draw is supposed to decline by $1,000 per month, the internal record should show approximately $9,000 remaining after three months. If the balance is still $11,000, the borrower is behind schedule. The homeowner can respond by increasing payments, reducing other spending, extending the deadline cautiously, or identifying another repayment source.

A redraw moratorium may be necessary when the plan falls behind. Under this rule, no additional nonemergency borrowing is permitted until the delayed draw returns to its scheduled balance. This prevents one missed target from expanding into several overlapping obligations. The line remains available for a genuine emergency, but discretionary use stops until control is restored.

The rules should become more conservative as the draw period approaches its end. A borrower who has only one year remaining should hesitate to approve a draw requiring three years to repay. Once the line enters the repayment period, access may end and monthly payments may increase. New draws near the conversion date can magnify the payment shock and reduce the homeowner's ability to adapt.

The homeowner should know the approximate payment that may result when principal repayment begins. A draw that adds only $100 to an interest-only payment today may add substantially more during the repayment period because both principal and interest must be paid. The decision should consider the future payment structure rather than relying solely on the current minimum payment.

Redraw discipline ultimately protects the value created by earlier principal payments. A household can spend years reducing a HELOC balance and reverse that progress through a few poorly planned transactions. Written rules keep available credit in its proper role as conditional borrowing capacity. They allow the homeowner to use the line when the benefit is strong, the repayment source is credible, and the resulting obligation remains within the financial plan.

The objective is not to prohibit every redraw. The revolving feature is one of the primary reasons homeowners choose a HELOC. The objective is to ensure that borrowing serves the homeowner rather than controlling the household's future cash flow. A carefully structured redraw can solve a temporary problem or support a worthwhile project. An open-ended redraw can convert restored home equity into permanent debt.

The strongest redraw rule is simple enough to follow and strict enough to protect progress. The homeowner identifies an approved purpose, limits the amount, names the repayment source, sets a deadline, calculates the payment, stress-tests the rate, preserves the reserve, and remains below the internal balance ceiling. When these conditions are satisfied, the draw becomes part of an organized capital plan rather than an improvised financial reaction.

Practical Math Example: Comparing a Controlled Redraw With Open-Ended Borrowing

Consider homeowners Marcus and Elena, who have a HELOC with a $225,000 credit limit and an outstanding balance of $108,000. The line carries a variable annual interest rate of 10.40 percent, and three years remain in the draw period. Their lender shows approximately $117,000 of available credit, but Marcus and Elena have established an internal maximum balance of $125,000. Their self-approved borrowing capacity is therefore only $17,000.

The couple has spent the previous two years reducing the HELOC from $150,000 to $108,000. They want to preserve that progress while replacing an aging air-conditioning system and repairing damaged ductwork. The first contractor proposes a complete project costing $18,500. A second contractor identifies $13,000 of necessary work and $5,500 of optional efficiency upgrades that could be completed later.

Marcus and Elena apply their redraw rules. The necessary work qualifies because the system is failing and the home requires dependable cooling. The optional improvements may provide value but are not immediately required. They therefore approve a maximum draw of $13,000 rather than borrowing the full $18,500. This decision keeps the resulting balance at $121,000, which remains $4,000 below their internal ceiling of $125,000.

Before drawing the money, they identify the repayment source. Marcus expects a documented $9,000 net bonus in four months. After reviewing their budget, the couple also determines that it can direct $1,000 per month of regular surplus toward the draw. The planned bonus and four monthly principal payments should provide the full $13,000 required to eliminate the redraw within four months.

At a 10.40 percent annual rate, the approximate daily interest on the $13,000 draw is calculated by multiplying $13,000 by 0.104 and dividing by 365. The result is approximately $3.70 per day. If the entire $13,000 remained outstanding for four months, or approximately 120 days, it would generate an estimated $444 of interest. Because the couple plans to reduce the draw by $1,000 each month, the actual interest attributable to it should be lower.

The couple schedules the contractor's payment for the day the work is completed. The lender requires two business days to transfer HELOC funds, so Marcus initiates the draw two business days before the contractor's deadline. He does not draw the money several weeks in advance. Delaying the transaction until the funds are required minimizes the number of interest-accruing days.

After the $13,000 draw, the total HELOC balance rises from $108,000 to $121,000. At the original balance of $108,000, simplified monthly interest was approximately $936 because $108,000 multiplied by 10.40 percent and divided by twelve equals $936. At the new $121,000 balance, simplified monthly interest is approximately $1,048.67. The draw initially increases the estimated monthly interest by approximately $112.67.

Marcus and Elena's required payment during the draw period is primarily interest-only. If they paid only the estimated $1,048.67, the balance would remain near $121,000. To meet their plan, they must add $1,000 of principal. Their first total payment should therefore be approximately $2,048.67, subject to the lender's actual daily calculation and any fees.

After the first $1,000 principal payment, the balance falls to approximately $120,000. The portion attributable to the project declines from $13,000 to $12,000. At a 10.40 percent annual rate, simplified monthly interest on the total $120,000 balance is approximately $1,040. To reduce the project draw by another $1,000, the couple's next total payment should be approximately $2,040.

After the second principal payment, the total balance falls to approximately $119,000, and the tracked project balance declines to $11,000. Simplified monthly interest on the total balance becomes approximately $1,031.33. The couple again adds $1,000 of principal, making a total estimated payment of approximately $2,031.33.

After the third principal payment, the HELOC balance falls to approximately $118,000, and the project portion declines to $10,000. Simplified monthly interest on the total balance is approximately $1,022.67. Marcus and Elena make another $1,000 principal payment during the fourth month, bringing the total HELOC balance to approximately $117,000 and the project portion to $9,000.

Marcus then receives the expected $9,000 net bonus. Because the bonus was designated as the repayment source before the draw occurred, the couple sends the entire amount to the HELOC. The balance falls from approximately $117,000 to approximately $108,000. The air-conditioning redraw has been completely repaid, and the total balance has returned to the point at which it stood before the project.

The couple then directs another $2,000 from unrelated savings above its cash-reserve floor toward permanent principal reduction. The HELOC balance falls from $108,000 to $106,000. The project has been completed, the related borrowing has been repaid, and the long-term balance is now $2,000 lower than it was before the draw.

At the original $108,000 balance, simplified annual interest was approximately $11,232. At the new $106,000 balance, simplified annual interest is approximately $11,024. The permanent $2,000 reduction creates estimated annual savings of $208. More importantly, the temporary $13,000 draw did not become permanent debt because it had a defined amount, repayment source, monthly target, and deadline.

Marcus and Elena compare their controlled strategy with an open-ended alternative. Under the alternative, they would have accepted the $18,500 proposal, including the $5,500 of optional improvements. They would have made only the interest payment while waiting for the $9,000 bonus and would have used the bonus for other household purchases. Without a principal schedule, the full $18,500 draw could have remained outstanding for the entire year.

An $18,500 draw at 10.40 percent produces simplified annual interest of approximately $1,924. The controlled $13,000 draw, if it had remained outstanding for a full year, would have produced approximately $1,352 of interest. The smaller initial draw therefore avoids approximately $572 of potential annual interest before considering the accelerated repayment.

The greater difference comes from the repayment timeline. Because the controlled draw is gradually reduced and eliminated after four months, the couple pays interest on a declining project balance for a limited period. A simplified calculation can estimate the project-related interest by examining the approximate balances of $13,000, $12,000, $11,000, and $10,000 during the four months before the bonus repayment.

The average project balance during those four months is approximately $11,500. Multiplying $11,500 by 10.40 percent and then by four-twelfths produces estimated project interest of approximately $398.67. Exact interest would depend on payment dates and daily balances, but the estimate shows the approximate cost of the controlled borrowing period.

Under the open-ended alternative, the $18,500 draw remaining for twelve months would generate approximately $1,924 of interest. Subtracting the controlled estimate of $398.67 produces a difference of approximately $1,525.33 during the first year. The controlled plan also finishes with no remaining project debt, while the open-ended plan finishes with the full $18,500 still included in the HELOC balance.

Marcus and Elena also calculate the effect on their total balance. The controlled plan returns the HELOC to $108,000 and then reduces it to $106,000. The open-ended plan raises the balance from $108,000 to $126,500. This amount exceeds their internal ceiling of $125,000 by $1,500. The alternative would therefore violate their borrowing rule before accounting for any other draws.

At a total balance of $126,500 and a 10.40 percent rate, simplified monthly interest would be approximately $1,096.33. At the controlled plan's ending balance of $106,000, simplified monthly interest is approximately $918.67. The difference is approximately $177.66 per month, or about $2,131.92 per year if the balances and rate remain unchanged.

The couple then performs a rate stress test. If the HELOC rate rises from 10.40 percent to 12 percent, the controlled ending balance of $106,000 would produce simplified monthly interest of approximately $1,060. The open-ended balance of $126,500 would produce approximately $1,265 per month. The difference would rise to approximately $205 per month.

The stress test demonstrates that unresolved redraws become more expensive when rates increase. Marcus and Elena cannot control the lender's index, but they can control whether optional work is financed, how much is borrowed, and how quickly the draw is repaid. Their rules reduce both the current interest cost and their exposure to future rate changes.

Several months later, Elena wants to draw $7,000 for new furniture. Although the amount is below the lender's available credit, the expense does not pass the couple's redraw test. It is not urgent, there is no separate repayment source, and borrowing would slow their permanent HELOC reduction. They decide to save $700 per month and purchase the furniture with cash after ten months.

If they had borrowed $7,000 at 10.40 percent and repaid only $700 of principal per month, the draw would have taken ten months to eliminate and generated interest throughout that period. Using a simplified average balance of approximately $3,850 over ten months, the furniture draw could have generated around $333.67 of interest. Saving before purchasing avoids that interest and prevents another balance increase.

The couple's rules do not prevent all borrowing. They permitted the air-conditioning draw because it funded necessary work, remained below the internal ceiling, and had a dependable repayment plan. They rejected the furniture draw because it was discretionary and unsupported by a separate repayment source. The difference was not whether sufficient credit existed. The difference was whether the transaction strengthened or weakened their overall plan.

Marcus and Elena continue tracking the HELOC balance every month. Their next internal ceiling is $115,000, even though the current balance is only $106,000. This gives them $9,000 of controlled capacity for a genuine need. At the end of the year, they intend to reduce the ceiling again so that restored lender availability does not encourage larger borrowing.

The practical math demonstrates that controlled redrawing requires more than comparing the current minimum payment with the household budget. The borrower must calculate the draw's interest, monthly principal target, repayment deadline, total future balance, and exposure to higher rates. A draw that appears small in relation to the credit limit may still create years of interest if no repayment source exists.

By limiting the project to its necessary portion, repaying principal monthly, applying the bonus as planned, and refusing an unsupported discretionary draw, Marcus and Elena preserve the progress created by their earlier payments. Their HELOC remains available, but its flexibility is governed by rules. This structure allows them to use home equity when the need is justified while ensuring that every temporary increase is followed by a deliberate return to a lower balance.

Chapter 5

Managing Variable-Rate Risk During Paydown and Redraw

A HELOC provides flexibility because the homeowner can generally borrow, repay, and redraw funds during the draw period. That flexibility is often accompanied by a variable interest rate. The rate may change even when the borrower does not make another draw, and an increase can raise both the monthly interest charge and the amount required to keep the account current. A disciplined paydown-and-redraw strategy must therefore manage not only the principal balance but also the uncertainty created by future rate changes.

Many HELOC rates are built from two components: an index and a margin. The index is a market-based rate that can move over time, while the margin is an additional percentage established by the lender under the loan agreement. If the index is 7.50 percent and the lender's margin is 1.50 percent, the resulting HELOC rate may be 9 percent. If the index later rises to 8.50 percent while the margin remains unchanged, the rate may rise to 10 percent.

The margin does not ordinarily change in the same way as the index, but the borrower should review the agreement to understand how the rate is determined. The documents may also identify a rate floor, rate ceiling, adjustment frequency, introductory rate, and any limits on individual adjustments. A floor prevents the rate from falling below a specified level, while a ceiling or lifetime cap limits how high the rate may rise. These provisions influence the borrower's potential cost and should be understood before creating a long-term plan.

An introductory rate can make a HELOC appear less expensive during the first several months. Once the promotional period ends, the rate may adjust to the index plus the contractual margin. A borrower who evaluates affordability only during the introductory period may underestimate future interest. The paydown plan should use the expected regular rate and should also test a rate several percentage points higher.

The relationship between the rate and balance is direct. A higher rate applied to a larger balance creates a greater increase in interest expense than the same rate change applied to a smaller balance. If a homeowner owes $50,000, a two-percentage-point increase adds approximately $1,000 of annual interest before considering principal changes. If the homeowner owes $200,000, the same rate increase adds approximately $4,000 of annual interest. Principal reduction therefore limits both current interest and future exposure to rate increases.

This protection is one of the strongest reasons to continue paying principal during an interest-only draw period. A borrower who pays only accrued interest may maintain the same balance year after year. If rates rise, the monthly payment increases even though the debt has not grown. A borrower who steadily reduces principal may offset part or all of the payment increase because the higher rate is applied to a smaller amount.

Suppose a homeowner owes $150,000 at 8 percent. Simplified annual interest is approximately $12,000, and monthly interest is approximately $1,000. If the rate rises to 10 percent while the balance remains $150,000, annual interest increases to approximately $15,000, and monthly interest rises to approximately $1,250. The rate change adds approximately $250 per month.

If the homeowner reduces the balance to $120,000 before the rate rises, monthly interest at 10 percent is approximately $1,000. The borrower would then pay about the same monthly interest at the new 10 percent rate on the lower balance as was previously paid at 8 percent on the higher balance. The $30,000 principal reduction offsets the effect of the two-percentage-point rate increase in this simplified comparison.

This relationship can be used to establish a defensive paydown target. Instead of choosing a balance goal arbitrarily, the homeowner can determine how much principal must be repaid to keep interest near a preferred level if the rate increases. The borrower identifies the maximum manageable monthly interest charge, selects a stress-tested annual rate, and calculates the balance that would produce that payment.

If a homeowner wants monthly interest to remain near or below $1,000 and wants to prepare for a possible rate of 12 percent, the stress-tested balance would be approximately $100,000. This amount is found by multiplying the $1,000 monthly target by twelve and dividing by 12 percent. If the current balance is $130,000, the borrower would need to reduce principal by approximately $30,000 to reach that defensive target.

The stress-tested rate should be realistic but conservative. The homeowner does not need to assume an unlimited rate unless the agreement permits such an outcome. The borrower should review the contractual ceiling, recent account history, and household tolerance for payment increases. Testing the current rate plus two percentage points and the current rate plus four percentage points may provide a practical view of moderate and severe scenarios.

Rate stress testing should occur before every significant redraw. A $25,000 draw may add approximately $208.33 per month in interest at 10 percent.

At 12 percent, the same draw adds approximately $250 per month. At 14 percent, it adds approximately $291.67 per month. The borrower should confirm that the draw remains affordable under the higher test rate, not merely under the current rate displayed at the time of borrowing.

The repayment timeline should also be tested. If the homeowner intends to repay a $25,000 draw within one year, the borrower must pay an average of approximately $2,083.33 of principal per month in addition to interest. At a 10 percent rate, the first month's simplified interest on the draw is approximately $208.33. The first total payment attributable to that draw would therefore be approximately $2,291.66. If the rate rises to 14 percent, the first month's interest becomes approximately $291.67, increasing the required total to approximately $2,375.

A borrower may be able to absorb a higher interest-only payment but still fail to reduce principal. This is a common risk during rising-rate periods. More of the household's planned payment is consumed by interest, leaving less available for principal. If the homeowner intends to send a fixed total payment of $2,000 each month, a rate increase may slow the paydown even though the payment amount does not change.

For example, a $150,000 balance at 8 percent generates simplified monthly interest of $1,000. A fixed $2,000 payment would direct approximately $1,000 toward principal. At a 12 percent rate, the same balance generates approximately $1,500 of monthly interest. The fixed $2,000 payment would then reduce principal by only about $500. The rate increase cuts the approximate monthly principal reduction in half.

The borrower can respond in several ways. The total payment can be increased, the principal-reduction deadline can be extended, new draws can be suspended, discretionary expenses can be reduced, or surplus income can be redirected toward the line. The correct response depends on the household's financial capacity. The homeowner should recognize the change early rather than discovering months later that the balance has stopped declining.

A rate-trigger rule creates an automatic response. Under this system, the homeowner establishes actions that occur when the rate reaches specified levels. If the rate rises by one percentage point, the borrower may direct an additional $200 per month toward the HELOC. If it rises by two percentage points, the household may stop all nonessential redraws. If it rises by three percentage points, the borrower may compare fixed-rate alternatives or direct a predetermined portion of savings above the reserve floor toward principal.

The trigger amounts should be based on the actual balance. A one-percentage-point increase adds approximately $83.33 per month for every $100,000 outstanding. On a $200,000 balance, the same increase adds approximately $166.67 per month. A homeowner can calculate the effect of each potential increase and incorporate the resulting payment into the budget before the adjustment occurs.

The borrower should monitor the account rate every month. The rate may appear on the statement, online account, or lender notice. The homeowner should record the rate along with the balance, interest charged, payments, and draws. A rising rate combined with a rising balance requires immediate attention because both variables are moving in the wrong direction.

Paydown and redraw behavior becomes especially important during a high-rate period. A borrower may pay $10,000 toward principal, restore $10,000 of available credit, and then redraw the full amount for discretionary spending. The interest protection created by the payment disappears. When rates are high, the cost of reversing progress is greater because the redrawn principal immediately begins generating interest at the elevated rate.

A homeowner may create a stricter internal draw limit when rates rise. At a rate below 8 percent, the household may allow approved draws up to $20,000. At a rate between 8 and 10 percent, the maximum might fall to $12,000. Above 10 percent, draws may be limited to critical emergencies and expenses supported by near-term repayment sources. This system connects borrowing behavior to the changing cost of capital.

The borrower should also reduce the maximum repayment period for new draws when rates are high. Carrying a draw for five years at a double-digit rate can create substantial interest expense. A draw that cannot be repaid within twelve or eighteen months may be too large, too optional, or better suited to another financing structure. Shortening the repayment deadline reduces the time during which the borrower remains exposed to rate changes.

Fixed-rate conversion options may be available within some HELOCs. These features may allow the borrower to convert part of the variable balance into a fixed-rate segment with a defined repayment schedule. The fixed rate may be higher than the current variable rate at the time of conversion, but it can provide predictable payments and protect against future increases. The homeowner should compare the conversion rate, fees, term, prepayment provisions, and effect on future borrowing capacity.

A fixed-rate home equity loan, personal loan, or mortgage refinance may also be considered, but the comparison must include more than the stated rate. Closing costs, loan terms, payment structure, collateral, total interest, and the loss of revolving access can change the result. Replacing a HELOC with a fixed loan may reduce rate uncertainty while increasing the required principal payment. The borrower needs to determine whether the household can afford the new payment.

Refinancing the first mortgage to pay off the HELOC may appear attractive when it produces one payment, but it can extend the HELOC debt over a much longer term. A homeowner should calculate the total cost rather than focusing only on the monthly payment. A lower monthly payment achieved by stretching debt over 20 or 30 years may result in substantially more cumulative interest.

The cash-reserve floor should remain protected during a rate increase. Using all available savings to reduce the HELOC can lower interest, but it may leave the household unable to manage an emergency. The borrower can establish a rate-defense fund above the emergency reserve. This separate amount is earmarked for principal reduction if the rate reaches a predetermined threshold.

For example, a homeowner with a $40,000 emergency reserve and an additional $15,000 of unassigned savings may decide to pay $5,000 toward the HELOC immediately. The remaining $10,000 becomes a rate-defense fund. If the rate rises by two percentage points, the homeowner applies another $5,000. If it rises further, the final $5,000 can be used after reviewing upcoming expenses. This staged approach preserves flexibility while preparing for higher borrowing costs.

The homeowner must also consider the interaction between inflation, income, and interest rates. Higher rates may occur during periods when household expenses are also increasing. The borrower should not assume that future salary increases will fully absorb the HELOC payment change. A stress test should include both a higher interest payment and higher essential expenses.

Rental-property owners should evaluate whether rent increases can realistically offset rising HELOC costs. Lease terms, vacancy risk, maintenance expenses, property taxes, and insurance premiums may limit the amount of additional income available. Using optimistic future rents to justify a large redraw can leave the investor exposed if operating costs rise faster than revenue.

Business owners face similar risks. A HELOC draw may fund inventory, advertising, equipment, or expansion, but higher rates can reduce the profitability of the transaction. If a project is expected to produce a 12 percent return and the HELOC rate rises from 9 percent to 12 percent, the expected spread may disappear before accounting for taxes and risk. The owner should calculate the project's return under a higher borrowing rate and a lower revenue forecast.

The variable rate also influences whether temporary paydowns are worthwhile. When the HELOC rate is high, applying excess cash for even several months can produce meaningful savings. A $50,000 temporary principal reduction at 12 percent saves approximately $500 per month while it remains applied. However, the money should not be placed in the HELOC if it is needed for a known obligation and future access is uncertain.

The borrower should examine the loan's maximum rate when planning for the end of the draw period. A variable balance that converts to principal-and-interest payments at a high rate can create a severe payment increase. The homeowner must consider both the rate risk and the amortization risk. Reducing principal before the repayment period limits the size of the balance that must be amortized.

A HELOC rate-management plan should be reviewed at least quarterly and whenever the rate changes. The homeowner records the current balance, current rate, monthly interest, remaining draw period, internal balance ceiling, reserve amount, and projected payment at higher rates. This review transforms rate changes from unexpected events into manageable adjustments.

The borrower cannot guarantee future rates, but uncertainty does not prevent preparation. Principal reduction, redraw limits, stress-tested payments, rate triggers, and protected cash reserves give the homeowner several ways to reduce exposure. Each dollar of permanent paydown lowers the amount affected by future adjustments. Each unnecessary redraw increases that amount.

The most important principle is that a low current payment should not be confused with long-term affordability. An interest-only minimum payment can rise quickly when rates increase, and it does not eliminate the balance. A homeowner who prepares only for today's payment may be forced to react under pressure later. A homeowner who stress-tests the line can reduce principal while choices remain available.

Managing variable-rate risk requires the borrower to coordinate mathematics with behavior. The homeowner calculates how much each rate increase will cost, establishes a balance target that supports an affordable payment, restricts new draws when rates become expensive, and reviews alternatives before the draw period ends. Through this process, the HELOC remains flexible without allowing the variable rate to control the household's financial future.

Practical Math Example: Stress-Testing a HELOC Under Rising Rates

Consider homeowners Steven and Natalie, who have a HELOC with a $240,000 credit limit and an outstanding balance of $175,000. The current annual interest rate is 8.75 percent, and the minimum payment during the draw period is based primarily on accrued interest. Five years remain in the draw period. The couple wants to reduce interest while retaining access to part of the line for necessary home and business expenses.

At the current 8.75 percent rate, simplified annual interest on the $175,000 balance is calculated by multiplying $175,000 by 0.0875. The result is $15,312.50. Dividing by twelve produces a simplified monthly interest estimate of approximately $1,276.04. This amount does not include fees, daily-balance differences, or principal reduction.

Steven and Natalie can afford a total HELOC payment of $2,500 per month. At the current rate and balance, approximately $1,276.04 of the payment would cover interest, leaving approximately $1,223.96 for principal during the first month. If the balance and rate remained unchanged, the simplified annual principal reduction would be approximately $14,687.52. In practice, interest would gradually decline as principal falls, allowing slightly more of the fixed payment to reduce the balance.

The couple first tests a rate of 10.75 percent, which is two percentage points above the current rate. At a $175,000 balance, simplified annual interest would be $18,812.50. Simplified monthly interest would rise to approximately $1,567.71. Their fixed $2,500 payment would then direct only approximately $932.29 toward principal during the first month.

The two-percentage-point rate increase raises estimated monthly interest by approximately $291.67. It also reduces the first month's principal payment by the same amount because the total payment remains fixed. At the current rate, approximately 48.96 percent of the $2,500 payment reaches principal. At the higher rate, only about 37.29 percent reaches principal during the first month.

Steven and Natalie next test a rate of 12.75 percent, which is four percentage points above the current rate. At that rate, simplified annual interest on $175,000 would be $22,312.50. Monthly interest would be approximately $1,859.38. Their fixed $2,500 payment would reduce principal by only approximately $640.62 during the first month.

Compared with the current rate, the 12.75 percent scenario increases estimated monthly interest by approximately $583.34. The principal portion of the fixed payment falls from approximately $1,223.96 to approximately $640.62. Without an adjustment, their paydown speed would be reduced by nearly half.

The couple establishes a maximum preferred monthly interest amount of $1,300. They want to determine the balance that would keep interest near or below that amount at the stress-tested rate of 12.75 percent. They multiply the $1,300 monthly limit by twelve, producing $15,600 of annual interest. They then divide $15,600 by 12.75 percent. The resulting defensive balance target is approximately $122,352.94.

Their current balance is $175,000, so they would need to reduce principal by approximately $52,647.06 to reach the defensive target. This amount is substantial, and they do not have enough surplus cash to pay it immediately. They decide to create a staged plan that uses an initial principal payment, larger monthly payments, and temporary restrictions on redrawing.

Steven and Natalie have $78,000 in savings. After analyzing essential expenses and known obligations, they establish a cash-reserve floor of $50,000. This leaves $28,000 above the reserve. Rather than applying the entire surplus, they make an initial $20,000 principal payment and retain an $8,000 rate-defense fund.

The $20,000 payment reduces the HELOC balance from $175,000 to $155,000. At the current 8.75 percent rate, simplified annual interest becomes $13,562.50, and monthly interest becomes approximately $1,130.21. Compared with the original monthly estimate of $1,276.04, the payment saves approximately $145.83 per month at the current rate.

The couple then repeats the higher-rate tests using the lower balance. At 10.75 percent, simplified monthly interest on $155,000 is approximately $1,388.54. At 12.75 percent, simplified monthly interest is approximately $1,646.88. The principal payment lowers the monthly interest under the severe rate scenario by approximately $212.50 compared with leaving the balance at $175,000.

Steven and Natalie continue making their fixed $2,500 monthly payment. At the current 8.75 percent rate and the new $155,000 balance, the first month's simplified interest is approximately $1,130.21, leaving approximately $1,369.79 for principal. The initial $20,000 payment therefore improves both the monthly interest cost and the portion of the fixed payment that reaches principal.

They also create a rate trigger. If the rate reaches 10.75 percent, they will apply $4,000 of the $8,000 rate-defense fund to principal and suspend nonemergency draws. If the rate reaches 12.75 percent, they will apply the remaining $4,000 after confirming that their cash reserve and upcoming expenses remain protected.

Six months later, the rate increases from 8.75 percent to 10.75 percent. During the previous six months, Steven and Natalie have reduced principal by approximately $8,300 through their fixed payments. The exact amount would depend on daily interest and the declining balance, but the simplified estimate brings the balance from $155,000 to approximately $146,700.

The couple activates the first trigger and applies $4,000 from the rate-defense fund. The balance falls to approximately $142,700. At 10.75 percent, simplified annual interest on this balance is approximately $15,340.25, and monthly interest is approximately $1,278.35. Their $2,500 total payment would direct approximately $1,221.65 toward principal during the next month.

The rate has risen by two percentage points, yet their estimated monthly interest of $1,278.35 is close to the original $1,276.04 amount they paid on the $175,000 balance at 8.75 percent. Their principal reduction has almost completely offset the effect of the rate increase.

If they had made no initial principal payment, no monthly principal reductions, and no rate-trigger payment, the $175,000 balance at 10.75 percent would have generated approximately $1,567.71 of monthly interest. Their strategy reduces that estimate by approximately $289.36 per month. It also leaves more of the fixed $2,500 payment available for principal.

Steven and Natalie are then offered an opportunity to redraw $25,000 for a home renovation. At the current 10.75 percent rate, the draw would add approximately $223.96 of simplified monthly interest. Their balance would rise from approximately $142,700 to $167,700, and total monthly interest would become approximately $1,502.29.

Their fixed $2,500 payment would then reduce principal by only approximately $997.71 during the first month. The renovation would also reverse much of their earlier progress and place them farther from the defensive balance target. Because the work is largely cosmetic and does not have a separate repayment source, they reject the draw.

Instead, they save $2,000 per month for the renovation. After twelve months, they will have $24,000 in cash and can decide whether to complete the project, reduce its scope, or continue saving. During the same period, their HELOC payments continue lowering principal. Avoiding the redraw prevents approximately $2,687.50 of annual interest at the 10.75 percent rate if the full $25,000 would otherwise have remained outstanding for the year.

Four months later, the rate rises again to 12.75 percent. During those four months, their simplified principal reductions total approximately $4,900, bringing the balance from $142,700 to approximately $137,800. They review their reserve and determine that it remains sufficient, so they apply the remaining $4,000 from the rate-defense fund. The balance falls to approximately $133,800.

At a 12.75 percent rate, simplified annual interest on $133,800 is approximately $17,059.50. Monthly interest is approximately $1,421.63. Their fixed $2,500 payment now directs approximately $1,078.37 toward principal during the first month at the higher rate.

If they had taken no action and still owed $175,000, monthly interest at 12.75 percent would be approximately $1,859.38. Their lower balance reduces the estimated monthly interest by approximately $437.75.

Although the rate is four percentage points higher than when the plan began, their monthly interest has increased by only about $145.59 compared with the original $1,276.04 estimate.

The couple has not yet reached its $122,352.94 defensive target, but it is now approximately $11,447.06 away. If the $2,500 payment continues and first-month principal reduction remains near $1,078, the balance can move toward the target over approximately eleven months. The actual period may be slightly shorter if interest declines as principal falls and the rate does not increase again.

Steven and Natalie calculate what will happen once the balance reaches approximately $122,353. At 12.75 percent, simplified monthly interest would be about $1,300, matching their preferred ceiling. A $2,500 total payment would then direct approximately $1,200 toward principal during the first month. Their progress would continue accelerating as the balance and interest charge declined.

They compare their strategy with a no-paydown scenario after the full rate increase. The no-paydown balance of $175,000 at 12.75 percent produces approximately $1,859.38 of monthly interest. Their targeted balance of approximately $122,353 produces approximately $1,300. The difference is approximately $559.38 per month, or $6,712.56 per year.

They also compare available credit. At the original $175,000 balance on a $240,000 line, they had approximately $65,000 available. At the target balance of approximately $122,353, they would have approximately $117,647 available. However, they do not treat this restored availability as permission to borrow. Their internal balance ceiling is reduced to $135,000, giving them less than $13,000 of self-approved emergency capacity once the target is reached.

This internal ceiling prevents future redraws from recreating the rate exposure they worked to eliminate. If they were to redraw the entire lender-approved $117,647, the balance could return to the $240,000 credit limit. At 12.75 percent, a $240,000 balance would generate simplified monthly interest of approximately $2,550, exceeding their entire current payment budget before any principal reduction.

The comparison shows why lender-approved capacity and borrower-approved capacity must remain separate. The lender may permit a much larger balance, but Steven and Natalie's budget cannot support that balance under the stress-tested rate. Their personal ceiling is based on affordable interest and long-term goals rather than the maximum amount displayed on the statement.

Through initial paydown, monthly principal payments, rate triggers, redraw restrictions, and stress testing, the couple maintains control during a significant rate increase. The rate rises from 8.75 percent to 12.75 percent, yet the balance reduction limits the increase in monthly interest. Their calculations allow them to respond according to a plan instead of reacting after the payment becomes unmanageable.

The practical lesson is that principal reduction acts as a defense against variable-rate risk. Every dollar removed from the balance is a dollar that will not be charged the next rate adjustment. A homeowner cannot predict exactly when rates will change, but the borrower can calculate the effect, establish triggers, protect cash reserves, and restrict redraws that would create excessive exposure. By managing both the balance and the rate risk, the homeowner can preserve access to capital without allowing future interest adjustments to erase the benefits of earlier paydown.

[illegible]

A HELOC paydown-and-redraw strategy must account for the date when the draw period ends. During the draw period, the homeowner may be able to borrow, repay, and borrow again up to the approved credit limit. The required payment may also be relatively low if it is based primarily on accrued interest. When the draw period expires, additional borrowing normally stops, and the outstanding balance enters a repayment period. The borrower may then be required to make principal-and-interest payments large enough to eliminate the debt over the remaining loan term.

This transition can produce one of the most significant financial changes associated with a HELOC. A homeowner may become accustomed to an interest-only payment that appears manageable. Even if [illegible] the original balance remains high once repayment begins, the monthly obligation may increase substantially because the borrower must pay interest and repay principal at the same time. If the rate is also variable, a higher index could add to the payment increase.

The first step in preparing for the transition is to identify the exact draw-period expiration date. The homeowner should not rely on a general memory that the line has "a few years left." The closing documents, monthly statements, and online account may identify the draw-period end date, repayment period length, and payment method. If the information is unclear, the borrower should contact the servicer and request a written explanation.

Chapter 6

Preparing for the End of the HELOC Draw Period

A HELOC paydown-and-redraw strategy must eventually account for the date on which the draw period ends. During the draw period, the homeowner may be able to borrow, repay, and borrow again up to the approved credit limit. The required payment may also be relatively low if it is based primarily on accrued interest. When the draw period expires, additional borrowing normally stops, and the outstanding balance enters a repayment period. The borrower may then be required to make principal-and-interest payments large enough to eliminate the debt over the remaining loan term.

This transition can produce one of the most significant financial changes associated with a HELOC. A homeowner may become accustomed to an interest-only payment that appears manageable even though the principal balance remains high. Once repayment begins, the monthly obligation may increase substantially because the borrower must pay interest and repay principal at the same time. If the rate is also variable, a higher index can magnify the payment increase.

The first step in preparing for the transition is to identify the exact draw-period expiration date. The homeowner should not rely on a general memory that the line has "a few years left." The closing documents, monthly statements, and online account may identify the draw-period end date, repayment-period length, and payment method. If the information is unclear, the borrower should contact the servicer and request a written explanation.

The borrower should also determine whether the end of the draw period occurs automatically or whether the lender offers any renewal, extension, refinance, or conversion option. A renewal should never be assumed. Even if the lender currently offers extensions, the borrower may need to requalify based on credit, income, property value, loan-to-value ratio, or other requirements. Market conditions and lender programs may also change before the current draw period expires.

The repayment structure should be reviewed carefully. Some HELOCs amortize the outstanding balance over ten, fifteen, or twenty years after the draw period. Others may require a shorter repayment schedule, a balloon payment, or another structure described in the agreement. The length of the repayment term greatly affects the monthly payment. A shorter term generally creates a higher required payment but may reduce total interest if the debt is repaid faster.

A homeowner should calculate the approximate repayment-period payment well before the transition. Waiting until the first principal-and-interest statement arrives can leave too little time to adjust. The borrower should estimate payments at the current balance and rate, a lower target balance, and one or more higher stress-tested rates. These scenarios reveal how much principal should be reduced before the conversion date.

Consider a homeowner who owes $150,000 at 10 percent and currently pays approximately $1,250 per month in interest. If the line converts into a fifteen-year amortizing repayment schedule at the same rate, the principal-and-interest payment may rise to approximately $1,612 per month. If the repayment term is ten years, the payment may rise to approximately $1,982 per month. The actual payment depends on the loan agreement, rate, and lender calculation, but the comparison demonstrates why the remaining term matters.

A shorter repayment period can create a much larger payment shock than the borrower expects. The homeowner may focus on the fact that the balance and rate have not changed, yet the required payment rises because principal must now be repaid on a schedule. The same $150,000 balance that produced a $1,250 interest-only payment may require several hundred dollars more each month after conversion.

If the rate rises before or during the repayment period, the payment can increase further. A $150,000 balance amortized over fifteen years at 12 percent requires an approximate principal-and-interest payment of $1,800 per month. Over ten years, the approximate payment would be $2,152. The borrower should therefore prepare for the combined effect of amortization and rate risk rather than examining either factor separately.

Principal reduction before conversion can significantly reduce the future payment. If the homeowner lowers the balance from $150,000 to $100,000, an approximate fifteen-year payment at 10 percent falls from about $1,612 to about $1,075. The $50,000 paydown reduces the estimated payment by more than $500 per month. It also reduces total interest because fewer dollars remain outstanding throughout the repayment period.

The value of principal reduction increases as the conversion date approaches because the borrower may soon lose the ability to redraw the repaid amount. During the earlier draw years, a homeowner may use temporary paydowns to lower interest while preserving conditional access to capital. Near the end of the draw period, principal payments should increasingly be viewed as permanent. Money needed after the conversion should remain in cash because repaid principal may no longer be accessible.

The cash-reserve floor should therefore be reevaluated before the draw period ends. A household that previously relied partly on available HELOC credit for contingency capacity may need to build a larger cash reserve. The borrower should not use every available dollar to reduce the balance and then discover that the line no longer permits draws. Preparing for repayment requires lowering principal while simultaneously preserving sufficient liquidity.

The household should calculate the difference between the current HELOC payment and the projected repayment-period payment. This difference represents the amount that must be absorbed by the monthly budget. If the current payment is $1,200 and the projected payment is $1,700, the budget must create an additional $500 per month. The homeowner can prepare by reducing discretionary expenses, increasing income, paying off other obligations, or beginning to make the higher payment before it becomes mandatory.

Practicing the future payment can be an effective preparation method. If the current required payment is $1,200 and the projected payment is $1,700, the homeowner can begin paying $1,700 now. The required interest is satisfied, and the additional $500 reduces principal. The borrower becomes accustomed to the future cash-flow requirement while lowering the balance that will eventually be amortized.

This practice creates a beneficial cycle. The homeowner's budget adapts to the higher payment, principal declines, current interest falls, and the projected repayment-period payment may become smaller. By the time the conversion occurs, the actual payment may be closer to the amount the household has already been paying voluntarily.

A borrower with several years remaining can establish annual balance milestones. Suppose a homeowner owes $180,000 and has four years left in the draw period. The household might target a balance of $155,000 after the first year, $130,000 after the second, $105,000 after the third, and $80,000 before conversion. These targets create a structured decline rather than leaving the entire problem for the final year.

Each annual target should be converted into monthly or quarterly principal goals. Reducing the balance by $25,000 in one year requires an average principal reduction of approximately $2,083 per month. If the borrower expects a $10,000 annual bonus, the monthly goal could be lowered by planning to apply the bonus to principal. However, the homeowner should maintain an alternative plan in case the bonus is smaller or does not occur.

Irregular income can be incorporated into the schedule through percentage rules. A business owner might direct 30 percent of every distribution above a minimum amount toward HELOC principal. A commissioned employee may dedicate half of each commission above the normal monthly budget. The borrower should still establish a minimum regular payment so that progress does not depend entirely on unpredictable income.

The homeowner should reduce redraw activity as the expiration date approaches. New draws during the final years increase the balance that must soon be amortized. A draw made six months before conversion may be followed almost immediately by higher principal-and-interest payments, and the borrower may lose the ability to repay and reuse the principal. The closer the expiration date becomes, the stronger the purpose and repayment source should be before any new borrowing is approved.

An internal redraw schedule can tighten over time. With more than three years remaining, the borrower may permit approved draws that can be repaid within twelve months. With two years remaining, the maximum repayment period may fall to six months. During the final year, the homeowner may prohibit nonemergency draws entirely. This gradual restriction prevents last-minute borrowing from reversing the paydown plan.

The borrower should also lower the internal HELOC balance ceiling. If the lender's credit limit is $250,000 and the homeowner owes $140,000, an internal ceiling of $150,000 may appear reasonable early in the draw period. As conversion approaches, the ceiling might fall to $130,000, then $110,000, and eventually to the target repayment balance. The decreasing ceiling ensures that restored credit is not mistaken for spendable wealth.

Known future expenses should be separated from the HELOC before the draw period ends. If the homeowner expects to replace a roof, pay tuition, purchase business equipment, or complete a necessary repair after the conversion date, the expense should be funded in cash or addressed while financing options remain available. The borrower should not assume that a new HELOC, refinance, or personal loan will be obtainable later.

Preparing for conversion also involves reviewing other debts. Paying off a car loan, credit card, or personal loan before the HELOC enters repayment may create room in the monthly budget. However, the homeowner should compare interest rates, remaining terms, collateral risk, and required payments. Eliminating a lower-rate debt solely to free cash flow may not produce the greatest interest savings, but it may still improve the household's ability to absorb the future HELOC payment.

A payment-shock reserve can provide additional protection. This reserve is separate from the general emergency fund and is intended to cover the difference between the expected and actual HELOC payment during the first several repayment months. If the projected increase is $600 per month, the homeowner might set aside $3,600 to cover six months of the difference. This provides time to adjust if the final payment is higher than estimated.

The borrower should examine whether the HELOC rate will remain variable during repayment. If it does, the payment may continue changing after conversion. A plan based solely on the first principal-and-interest payment may underestimate future costs. The homeowner should calculate payments at the current rate, a moderately higher rate, and the contractual maximum if that scenario is reasonably possible.

A fixed-rate conversion may be considered before the draw period ends if the HELOC offers that feature. Converting part of the balance may provide payment certainty, but the borrower must compare the fixed rate, term, fees, and payment with the variable alternative. The fixed segment may also reduce the amount available for future draws. The decision should be based on the complete cost and the household's need for predictability.

Refinancing into a home equity loan or another fixed-rate product may also reduce uncertainty. However, approval is not guaranteed, and the new loan may include closing costs, higher required payments, or a longer repayment term. The borrower should begin reviewing alternatives well before the HELOC expires so that decisions are not made under deadline pressure.

A new HELOC should not be used automatically to restart the cycle. Replacing an expiring line with a fresh interest-only draw period may lower the immediate payment, but it can postpone principal repayment for many more years. If the homeowner continues redrawing, the debt may remain attached to the property indefinitely. A renewal should support a defined financial strategy rather than merely avoid the consequences of the original repayment schedule.

The borrower should compare the cost of keeping the existing repayment plan with the cost of refinancing. The comparison should include the new rate, fees, appraisal costs, annual charges, repayment term, total projected interest, and effect on available equity. A lower rate may not produce a better result if the debt is extended over a much longer period and only minimum payments are made.

Credit qualification should also be addressed early. If the homeowner expects to refinance before the draw period ends, credit scores, debt-to-income ratios, employment history, income documentation, and property condition may affect approval. Waiting until the final month can be risky if credit improvement, document preparation, repairs, or appraisal issues require additional time.

Self-employed borrowers may need even more preparation. Income shown on tax returns, business bank statements, profit-and-loss statements, or other records can vary significantly. A borrower who qualified for the original HELOC may not qualify for a replacement under future guidelines. Maintaining organized records and protecting credit can preserve more options, but the safest plan is one that does not depend entirely on obtaining new financing.

Property value is another uncertain factor. A homeowner may assume that rising equity will support a new HELOC or refinance, but real estate values can decline. A lower appraisal can reduce the amount available or prevent approval. Paying down the existing balance improves the combined loan-to-value position and reduces dependence on future appreciation.

The homeowner should request a projected repayment schedule from the servicer when possible. This schedule may show the expected payment based on the current balance and rate. The borrower should remember that the projection can change if additional draws occur or the variable rate adjusts. It is a planning tool, not a guaranteed future payment.

Statements should be reviewed for any notice about upcoming changes. Lenders may send information months before the draw period ends. Ignoring these notices can result in missed deadlines or lost opportunities to select a repayment option. The homeowner should preserve copies of all correspondence and verify any required action directly with the servicer.

A final-year plan should become increasingly conservative. The borrower should know the target balance, projected payment, cash reserve, payment-shock reserve, remaining approved draws, and financing alternatives. Nonessential borrowing should generally stop, and all surplus above protected reserves should be considered for principal reduction. The household should already be practicing the anticipated repayment payment.

The end of the draw period does not need to become a financial crisis. It becomes dangerous when the borrower ignores the deadline, carries a large balance, depends on interest-only payments, and assumes another lender will provide a replacement line. Early preparation transforms the conversion into a planned stage of debt repayment.

The objective of the paydown-and-redraw strategy is not merely to maximize available credit during the draw period. It is to use the flexibility of the line while moving toward a balance that remains affordable when that flexibility ends. Every principal payment made before conversion lowers interest, reduces the future required payment, and decreases the household's dependence on refinancing.

By identifying the conversion date, projecting the new payment, stress-testing higher rates, establishing annual balance targets, limiting redraws, preserving cash, and reviewing financing alternatives early, the homeowner can approach the repayment period with control. The draw period is temporary, but the consequences of the ending balance can last for many years. The strongest strategy prepares for that reality long before the final draw is made.

Practical Math Example: Reducing Payment Shock Before the Draw Period Ends

Consider homeowners Carlos and Diana, who have a HELOC with a $250,000 credit limit and an outstanding balance of $180,000. The current variable interest rate is 10 percent. Their draw period ends in three years, and the remaining balance will then be amortized over a fifteen-year repayment period. During the draw period, their required payment is based primarily on accrued interest.

At the current $180,000 balance and 10 percent rate, simplified annual interest is approximately $18,000. Dividing by twelve produces a current interest-only payment estimate of $1,500 per month. Carlos and Diana have become comfortable making this payment, but it does not materially reduce the principal.

If the $180,000 balance enters a fifteen-year repayment period at the same 10 percent rate, the approximate principal-and-interest payment would be $1,934 per month. The estimated payment increase is therefore approximately $434 per month. This represents an increase of almost 29 percent even though the balance and rate remain unchanged.

Carlos and Diana also test a 12 percent rate. If the balance remains $180,000 and the repayment term is fifteen years, the approximate principal-and-interest payment would be $2,160 per month. Compared with the current $1,500 interest-only payment, this would create an estimated monthly increase of approximately $660.

They then test a more severe rate of 14 percent. At that rate, a $180,000 balance amortized over fifteen years would require an approximate payment of $2,397 per month. The increase over the current interest-only payment would be approximately $897 per month. The couple recognizes that maintaining the existing balance exposes the household to a significant payment shock.

Carlos and Diana decide that they want the repayment-period payment to remain below approximately $1,600 per month, even if the rate reaches 12 percent. They calculate the approximate balance that a $1,600 payment could support over fifteen years at 12 percent. Based on the amortization formula, the target balance is approximately $133,300.

Their current balance is $180,000, so they need to reduce principal by approximately $46,700 during the remaining three-year draw period. Dividing $46,700 by 36 months produces an average required principal reduction of approximately $1,297.22 per month.

At the current 10 percent rate, the simplified first month's interest on the $180,000 balance is $1,500. To reduce principal by approximately $1,297.22 during that month, Carlos and Diana need to make a total payment of approximately $2,797.22. They round the planned payment to $2,800 per month.

This payment is substantially higher than the current $1,500 requirement, but it serves two purposes. It allows the couple to practice making a payment close to or above the amount that may be required during repayment, and the difference reduces principal. As the balance declines, the interest portion should also decline if the rate remains unchanged, allowing more of the fixed $2,800 payment to reach principal.

During the first month, approximately $1,500 covers interest and $1,300 reduces principal. The balance falls from $180,000 to approximately $178,700. In the second month, simplified interest on the lower balance is approximately $1,489.17. A $2,800 payment then reduces principal by approximately $1,310.83, bringing the balance to approximately $177,389.17.

The amount reaching principal increases slightly each month because interest is calculated on a declining balance. If the rate remains at 10 percent and Carlos and Diana continue paying $2,800 per month, they may reach the $133,300 target before the full 36 months have passed. The exact result depends on the lender's daily interest calculations and any rate changes.

The couple expects to receive a $12,000 net work bonus after the first year. They do not depend on the bonus to make the minimum plan work, but they intend to apply it to principal if it is received. The bonus creates a margin of safety against rate increases, income fluctuations, or unexpected expenses.

Using a simplified projection, assume their regular payments reduce principal by approximately $16,000 during the first year. The balance would fall from $180,000 to approximately $164,000. When the $12,000 bonus is applied, the balance falls further to approximately $152,000.

At a $152,000 balance and 10 percent rate, simplified monthly interest is approximately $1,266.67. A fixed payment of $2,800 would then direct approximately $1,533.33 toward principal during the next month. The bonus improves the monthly allocation because interest is now calculated on a substantially lower balance.

Carlos and Diana continue paying $2,800 per month during the second year. Using a simplified estimate of approximately $19,000 in principal reduction, the balance falls from $152,000 to approximately $133,000 by the end of that year. They reach the original defensive target with approximately one year remaining in the draw period.

At a $133,000 balance and 10 percent rate, the current simplified interest-only charge is approximately $1,108.33 per month. If the balance enters a fifteen-year repayment period at 10 percent, the approximate principal-and-interest payment would be about $1,429 per month. At 12 percent, the approximate payment would be about $1,596 per month.

Their paydown therefore achieves the intended objective. At the stress-tested 12 percent rate, the projected payment remains close to their $1,600 ceiling. Compared with the approximate $2,160 payment on the original $180,000 balance at 12 percent, the lower balance reduces the projected payment by approximately $564 per month.

Carlos and Diana still have one year remaining before conversion. They could reduce their $2,800 payment to the projected repayment amount, but they decide to continue paying $2,800 while income remains stable. This allows them to lower the balance further and creates additional protection against higher rates.

Assume the rate rises to 11 percent during the final year. At a $133,000 balance, simplified monthly interest becomes approximately $1,219.17.

Their $2,800 payment initially reduces principal by approximately $1,580.83. As the balance declines, the principal portion grows.

Using a conservative simplified estimate, the couple reduces principal by another $19,500 during the final year. The balance at conversion falls from approximately $133,000 to approximately $113,500. This is $66,500 below the original $180,000 balance.

If the repayment-period rate is 11 percent and the $113,500 balance is amortized over fifteen years, the approximate monthly principal-and-interest payment would be $1,290. This payment is lower than the $1,500 interest-only payment they were making at the beginning of the plan.

The result demonstrates how aggressive preparation can reverse the expected payment shock. If Carlos and Diana had made only interest payments, their approximate repayment payment at 11 percent on $180,000 would have been about $2,046 per month. By reducing the balance to $113,500, they lower that projected payment by approximately $756 per month.

The couple also calculates the projected total interest during the fifteen-year repayment period. If they enter repayment owing $180,000 at 11 percent and make an approximate $2,046 monthly payment for 180 months, total payments would equal approximately $368,280. Subtracting the $180,000 principal produces approximate repayment-period interest of $188,280.

If they enter repayment owing $113,500 at the same 11 percent rate and make an approximate $1,290 monthly payment for 180 months, total payments would equal approximately $232,200. Subtracting the $113,500 principal produces approximate repayment-period interest of $118,700.

The lower starting balance reduces projected repayment-period interest by approximately $69,580.

These figures do not include the interest paid during the three-year preparation period, and actual lender calculations may differ. However, the comparison demonstrates the long-term effect of entering repayment with less principal. The benefit is not limited to a lower first payment. It continues throughout the amortization schedule.

Carlos and Diana also preserve a $45,000 cash reserve outside the HELOC. They do not use this money to reach the lower balance because they will soon lose redraw access. The cash allows them to manage emergencies after conversion without depending on a new loan.

During the final year, the couple creates a separate payment-shock reserve of $6,000. They originally expected that the required payment might rise by several hundred dollars. Although their principal reduction now suggests that the repayment payment may actually be lower than the original interest-only amount, they retain the reserve until the first several principal-and-interest statements confirm the actual payment.

They also stop all nonemergency draws. The lender shows approximately $136,500 of available credit when the balance reaches $113,500, but this amount will soon cease to be available. The couple does not interpret the unused line as an opportunity for last-minute spending.

Suppose they had made a $30,000 renovation draw shortly before conversion. The ending balance would have risen from $113,500 to $143,500. At 11 percent over fifteen years, the approximate repayment payment would have increased from about $1,290 to about $1,630 per month. The draw would therefore add approximately $340 to the required monthly payment.

The $30,000 draw would also create substantial long-term interest if carried for the full repayment term. An additional approximate payment of $340 over 180 months equals $61,200. Subtracting the $30,000 borrowed produces approximately $31,200 of additional interest attributable to the renovation under this simplified comparison.

Because the renovation is optional and does not have a separate repayment source, Carlos and Diana delay it. They plan to save cash after the repayment payment is confirmed. Their decision protects the balance reduction achieved during the previous three years.

The couple's strategy works because it begins well before the draw period expires. They calculate the expected payment shock, select a stress-tested payment ceiling, determine the necessary target balance, convert the target into monthly principal reductions, apply a bonus, practice making the higher payment, preserve cash, and stop unnecessary redraws.

If they had waited until the final six months, reducing principal by $66,500 would have required more than $11,000 per month before interest. Beginning three years earlier makes the target more manageable and allows declining interest to support additional principal reduction.

The practical lesson is that the ending balance is one of the most important numbers in a HELOC strategy. Available credit may matter during the draw period, but once that period ends, the outstanding balance determines the debt that must be amortized. A lower ending balance can reduce the future payment, decrease total interest, and limit the effect of higher rates.

By treating the draw-period expiration as a scheduled financial event rather than a distant deadline, a homeowner can make gradual adjustments while choices remain available. Carlos and Diana do not eliminate every financial risk, but they enter repayment with a lower balance, a manageable projected payment, preserved cash reserves, and no dependence on obtaining a replacement line. Their example shows how paydown discipline can turn a potentially disruptive HELOC conversion into a controlled transition toward complete repayment.

Chapter 7

Measuring True Progress With a HELOC Paydown-and-Redraw Review

A HELOC can generate a large amount of account activity without producing meaningful debt reduction. Money may enter the line through required payments, extra principal payments, bonuses, business income, or temporary deposits. Money may leave through planned redraws, emergency draws, transfers, convenience checks, or direct payments to vendors. If the homeowner focuses only on the amount paid into the account, the strategy can appear successful even when the outstanding balance is unchanged or rising. True progress must therefore be measured according to the net result after every payment and redraw has been considered.

The most important measurement is the change in principal balance over a meaningful period. A monthly review is useful for identifying immediate problems, while quarterly and annual reviews reveal the larger trend. If a homeowner begins the year owing $150,000 and finishes owing $125,000, the line has achieved a net principal reduction of $25,000. The number of transactions that occurred during the year does not change that result. If the homeowner paid $60,000 into the account but redrew $35,000 of principal, the net progress remains approximately $25,000 before accounting for any fees or capitalized charges.

This distinction prevents gross payments from being confused with net paydown. A borrower may proudly report paying $5,000 per month toward a HELOC. However, if approximately $1,200 covers interest and the borrower redraws $3,000 each month for expenses, only about $800 may reduce the balance. Over twelve months, the borrower may have transferred $60,000 into the line while achieving less than $10,000 of actual principal reduction.

The monthly statement contains much of the information required for an effective review, but the homeowner must interpret each category correctly. The beginning balance shows the amount owed at the start of the billing cycle. New advances or draws increase the amount owed. Interest and fees also increase the total obligation. Payments reduce the amount owed, although the payment is usually applied first to accrued interest, fees, or other required amounts before reducing principal. The ending balance reflects the combined result of these activities.

A basic balance equation can be expressed in paragraph form as follows: the ending balance is approximately equal to the beginning balance, plus new draws, plus interest and fees, minus total payments. If the loan statement reports a beginning balance of $100,000, new draws of $4,000, interest and fees of $900, and total payments of $6,000, the ending balance should be approximately $98,900. The borrower paid $6,000, but the actual balance declined by only $1,100 because draws and finance charges consumed the rest.

The principal portion of the payment should be calculated separately. If the total payment is $6,000 and $900 is applied to interest and fees, approximately $5,100 reaches principal. If the borrower also redraws $4,000, the net principal reduction is approximately $1,100. This calculation shows the difference between payment activity and permanent progress.

The homeowner should track permanent principal reduction separately from temporary paydowns. A permanent paydown represents money that the borrower intends to leave in the line. A temporary paydown represents cash placed against the balance for a limited period before a known redraw. Both can reduce interest while the balance remains lower, but only the permanent portion advances the long-term debt-reduction goal.

Suppose a business owner applies $30,000 to the HELOC after receiving a large customer payment. Of that amount, $12,000 represents permanent principal reduction, while $18,000 will be needed for taxes and operating expenses in three months. The full $30,000 lowers the balance temporarily, but the homeowner should not record the entire amount as permanent progress. The internal ledger should show $12,000 of permanent paydown and $18,000 of temporary paydown scheduled for future withdrawal.

When the $18,000 is later redrawn, the homeowner should not view the increase as an unexpected reversal. It was part of the original temporary-paydown plan. The strategy can still be successful because the money reduced the balance and generated interest savings during the three months it remained applied. However, the annual principal target should be evaluated using only the amount that remained in the line.

A redraw register provides a clear record of borrowed amounts. Each draw should be assigned a purpose, date, original amount, planned repayment source, scheduled repayment date, and remaining balance. Even though the lender combines all draws into one account balance, the homeowner's internal records can treat them as separate obligations. This prevents a planned business draw, home repair, and emergency expense from becoming one indistinguishable debt.

Every additional principal payment can then be allocated internally. If the homeowner pays $3,000 beyond the interest due, the borrower may assign $2,000 to a home-repair draw and $1,000 to permanent balance reduction.

The lender may not apply the payment according to these categories, but the internal allocation allows the homeowner to measure progress against each goal.

The monthly review should begin by recording the statement's opening and closing dates. This ensures that income, payments, draws, and interest are assigned to the correct period. A transaction initiated on the final day of the month may not post until the next billing cycle. Using statement dates rather than assumptions prevents errors when comparing balances.

The borrower should then record the opening principal balance, current interest rate, total interest charged, total fees, total payments, total new draws, ending balance, available credit, and remaining draw period. The homeowner should also record the cash-reserve balance because HELOC progress should not be achieved by weakening household liquidity below the established floor.

A decline in the HELOC balance accompanied by a decline in cash reserves may represent a transfer rather than financial improvement. If a homeowner lowers the HELOC by $20,000 but reduces savings by the same $20,000, net debt is lower, but liquidity is also lower. This may still be a sensible decision when cash exceeds the reserve requirement, but the household should understand the tradeoff. If the cash reserve falls below its floor, the payment may have been too aggressive.

The review should compare the ending balance with three benchmarks. The first is the previous month's ending balance, which shows short-term direction. The second is the balance at the beginning of the year, which shows cumulative progress. The third is the homeowner's planned target balance, which shows whether the strategy is ahead of or behind schedule.

Suppose a homeowner begins the year with a $144,000 balance and wants to reduce it to $120,000 by year-end. This requires a net principal reduction of $24,000, or an average of $2,000 per month. After three months, the planned balance would be approximately $138,000. If the actual balance is $140,500, the homeowner is $2,500 behind the planned schedule. The borrower can then adjust payments or restrict redraws before the gap becomes larger.

A temporary redraw does not necessarily mean the plan has failed. If the borrower is above the monthly target because of an approved draw that will be repaid by a documented bonus next month, the plan may remain intact. The homeowner should record both the actual balance and the adjusted projected balance after the expected repayment. Nevertheless, anticipated income should not be counted as received money, and the borrower should prepare for a delay.

The homeowner should calculate the redraw ratio to identify whether new borrowing is consuming too much of the principal repaid. This ratio compares total draws with gross principal payments over a period. If the borrower pays $30,000 of principal during the year and redraws $12,000, the redraw ratio is 40 percent. The net principal reduction is $18,000. A high ratio may indicate that the line is being used too frequently or that temporary paydowns are being mistaken for permanent progress.

The ratio must be interpreted in context. A high redraw ratio may be expected when the homeowner intentionally uses the HELOC to manage seasonal business cash flow. However, if the stated goal is rapid debt elimination, repeatedly redrawing most of the principal is inconsistent with that goal. The borrower should examine the purposes of the draws and determine whether they are necessary, productive, or discretionary.

Interest savings should also be measured. The homeowner can compare the current interest charge with the amount that would have been charged on the original balance at the current rate. Suppose the original balance was $150,000 and the current balance is $120,000. At a 10 percent rate, simplified monthly interest on the original balance would be $1,250, while interest on the current balance would be approximately $1,000. The $30,000 reduction creates estimated monthly savings of about $250.

The borrower should not compare interest charges across months without considering rate changes and the number of days in each billing cycle. A lower balance may still generate a higher interest charge if the rate increased. A month with 31 days may also produce more interest than a month with 28 days. To measure the effect of principal reduction accurately, the homeowner should calculate interest on both balances using the same rate and time period.

The effective direction of the line can be measured through a rolling three-month or six-month average. One month may contain a large planned draw or annual expense that temporarily increases the balance. A multi-month review reveals whether the account returns to its prior level and continues declining. If the balance rises across several consecutive review periods, the homeowner should identify the cause.

A rising balance may result from insufficient total payments, excessive redraws, increasing interest rates, new fees, or a household cash-flow deficit. Each cause requires a different response. If the required payment covers only interest, the borrower needs additional principal payments. If redraws are excessive, borrowing rules must be tightened. If the rate has risen, the total payment may need to increase. If recurring expenses exceed income, the household budget must be corrected.

The homeowner should measure the average cost of each draw. If a $10,000 draw remains outstanding for six months at 10 percent, its simplified interest cost is approximately $500. If the draw produces a measurable financial benefit greater than that amount, the borrowing may have served its intended purpose. If the money funds consumption without creating income, value, or necessary protection, the interest becomes an additional cost of the purchase.

The analysis should also include opportunity costs and transaction fees. A draw may include transfer fees, annual fees, early closure charges, fixed-rate conversion fees, or other expenses. The homeowner should add these costs to interest when evaluating the transaction. A low stated rate does not guarantee that a small or short-term draw is economical after fees are included.

Available credit should be tracked but should not become a performance goal by itself. An increase in available credit generally results from principal repayment, but its purpose is to preserve flexibility, not encourage borrowing. The homeowner should compare lender-approved availability with the household's internal borrowing capacity. If the line shows $100,000 available but the internal ceiling permits only $15,000 of additional borrowing, the review should emphasize the $15,000 figure.

The internal balance ceiling should decline according to the long-term plan. A homeowner might begin the year with a ceiling of $150,000 and reduce it by $5,000 each quarter. The account may permit a higher balance, but the borrower's rules prevent the line from returning to its previous level. Recording the ceiling each month creates a behavioral barrier against unnecessary redraws.

The remaining draw period should be included in every review. A balance of $100,000 with eight years of redraw access creates a different situation from the same balance with six months remaining. As the draw period shortens, temporary paydowns should be reduced, cash reserves should be strengthened, and nonessential draws should become less acceptable.

The projected repayment-period payment should be updated whenever the balance or rate changes. This number translates the current HELOC balance into a future monthly obligation. If the projected payment remains above the household's affordable level, principal targets may need to become more aggressive. If the payment falls below the target because of successful paydown, the homeowner gains additional flexibility.

The borrower should also measure progress in relation to home equity. If the property is worth $500,000, the first mortgage balance is $250,000, and the HELOC balance is $100,000, total secured debt is $350,000. The combined loan-to-value ratio is approximately 70 percent. If the HELOC balance falls to $75,000 and the property value remains constant, total secured debt falls to $325,000, and combined loan-to-value improves to approximately 65 percent.

Property appreciation should not be counted as a substitute for principal reduction. A rising property value can improve the combined loan-to-value ratio, but it does not reduce the dollars owed or the monthly interest charge. The homeowner cannot control future market values, while principal payments directly lower the debt. The review should therefore report both balance reduction and equity changes separately.

A quarterly review can examine broader decisions that do not need to be revisited every month. These include whether the cash-reserve floor remains appropriate, whether the internal redraw limit should be lowered, whether the rate requires a stronger paydown response, whether refinancing alternatives should be compared, and whether upcoming expenses may affect the plan.

An annual review should measure total payments, total interest, total draws, net principal reduction, ending cash reserves, and progress toward the draw-period target. This is also the appropriate time to establish the next year's balance ceiling and principal goal. If the previous target was missed, the homeowner should determine why before simply carrying the same strategy into another year.

The review process should remain simple enough to maintain. A homeowner does not need an elaborate accounting system if a monthly statement and basic worksheet provide the necessary information. The most important figures are the opening balance, ending balance, principal paid, amount redrawn, interest charged, cash reserve, and progress against the target. Complexity should support clarity rather than discourage regular review.

Behavioral observations belong in the review as well. The borrower should identify whether draws were planned or impulsive, whether the household followed the waiting period, whether repayment sources performed as expected, and whether available credit influenced spending decisions. Mathematics can show what happened, but behavioral review helps explain why it happened.

The homeowner should recognize positive progress without allowing one successful month to justify a new draw. A lower balance is not a reward account. The restored credit does not need to be used to validate the effort made. Progress becomes durable when the lower balance is allowed to remain lower.

A HELOC paydown-and-redraw review creates accountability. It shows whether payments are reducing debt, whether redraws are controlled, whether interest is declining, whether cash remains protected, and whether the borrower is prepared for the end of the draw period. Without this review, activity can obscure the true direction of the account.

The central measurement is simple: after accounting for interest, fees, and every redraw, is the principal balance moving downward at the planned rate? If the answer is yes and cash reserves remain protected, the strategy is producing measurable improvement. If the answer is no, the review identifies the gap early enough for the homeowner to respond.

Practical Math Example: Calculating Net HELOC Progress Over Twelve Months

Consider homeowners James and Olivia, who begin the year with a HELOC balance of $168,000 and a credit limit of $240,000. The line carries a variable rate of 9.80 percent, and four years remain in the draw period. Their year-end goal is to reduce the balance to $144,000, representing a planned net principal reduction of $24,000.

To reach the goal evenly, James and Olivia need to reduce principal by an average of $2,000 per month. Their monthly interest at the starting balance can be estimated by multiplying $168,000 by 9.80 percent and dividing by twelve. The result is approximately $1,372 per month. To reduce principal by $2,000 during the first month, their total payment must therefore be approximately $3,372, assuming no fees, new draws, or daily-balance differences.

During the first month, the couple makes a total payment of $3,500. The statement shows $1,372 of interest and no fees. Approximately $2,128 reaches principal, reducing the balance from $168,000 to $165,872. Because no draws occur, the entire $2,128 principal reduction is permanent progress.

During the second month, the simplified interest on the lower balance is approximately $1,354.62. The couple again pays $3,500, allowing approximately $2,145.38 to reduce principal. The ending balance falls to approximately $163,726.62. Their cumulative principal reduction after two months is approximately $4,273.38, placing them about $273 ahead of the planned $4,000 reduction.

In the third month, James receives a $10,000 business distribution. He and Olivia determine that $6,000 is true surplus and $4,000 will be needed for quarterly taxes in 60 days. They pay the full $10,000 into the HELOC, but their internal record classifies only $6,000 as permanent principal reduction. The other $4,000 is recorded as a temporary paydown.

Before the $10,000 payment, simplified monthly interest on the approximate $163,726.62 balance is $1,337.10. They make their normal $3,500 payment, reducing principal by approximately $2,162.90 and bringing the balance to approximately $161,563.72. They then apply the additional $10,000 distribution, lowering the statement balance to approximately $151,563.72.

The statement appears to show exceptional progress because the balance has declined by more than $12,000 during the month. However, James and Olivia's internal review separates the result. Approximately $8,162.90 represents permanent progress, consisting of the $2,162.90 regular principal reduction and the $6,000 permanent portion of the distribution. The remaining $4,000 is scheduled to be redrawn for taxes.

During the fourth month, no new draws occur. Simplified interest on the $151,563.72 balance is approximately $1,237.77. A $3,500 payment reduces principal by approximately $2,262.23, bringing the balance to approximately $149,301.49. The temporary $4,000 remains applied, so it continues lowering the average balance and saving interest.

During the fifth month, James redraws the $4,000 needed for taxes. Before the redraw, simplified interest is approximately $1,219.30. The couple makes another $3,500 payment, reducing principal by approximately $2,280.70 and lowering the balance to approximately $147,020.79. The $4,000 redraw then raises the ending balance to approximately $151,020.79.

A homeowner looking only at the fourth and fifth month-end balances might conclude that the plan moved backward because the balance rose from approximately $149,301.49 to $151,020.79. The internal ledger provides the correct interpretation. The $4,000 increase was a planned return of temporary funds, while the regular payment still created approximately $2,280.70 of permanent principal reduction.

The couple calculates the interest benefit produced by the temporary paydown. The $4,000 remained in the HELOC for approximately 60 days at a rate of 9.80 percent. Simplified savings are calculated by multiplying $4,000 by 9.80 percent and then multiplying by 60 divided by 365. The result is approximately $64.44. The temporary paydown did not create permanent debt reduction, but it generated a modest interest benefit while the money was not needed.

During the sixth month, the couple faces a $9,000 roof repair. The expense passes their redraw rules because it is necessary, the amount is supported by written estimates, and a repayment source has been identified. Olivia expects a $6,000 net bonus in three months, and the couple can direct an additional $1,000 per month toward the draw.

Before the roof draw, simplified monthly interest on the approximate $151,020.79 balance is $1,233.34. Their normal $3,500 payment reduces principal by approximately $2,266.66, bringing the balance to approximately $148,754.13. The $9,000 draw then increases the ending balance to approximately $157,754.13.

The statement balance is now higher than it was at the end of the previous month, but the couple does not combine the roof draw with permanent principal. Their ledger records a separate $9,000 roof-repair obligation with a three-month repayment schedule. They continue measuring ordinary principal reduction against the underlying balance while also tracking the remaining repair draw.

In the seventh month, simplified interest on the total $157,754.13 balance is approximately $1,288.33. James and Olivia make their regular $3,500 payment plus an additional $1,000 payment for the roof draw, for a total of $4,500. Approximately $3,211.67 reaches principal. They assign $1,000 to the roof-repair balance and approximately $2,211.67 to permanent paydown. The total HELOC balance falls to approximately $154,542.46, while the tracked roof draw falls to $8,000.

During the eighth month, simplified interest on $154,542.46 is approximately $1,262.10. They again pay $4,500, allowing approximately $3,237.90 to reach principal. They assign $1,000 to the roof obligation and approximately $2,237.90 to permanent paydown. The total balance falls to approximately $151,304.56, and the tracked roof draw falls to $7,000.

In the ninth month, Olivia receives the expected $6,000 bonus. Simplified interest on the total balance is approximately $1,235.65. The couple makes its normal $3,500 payment, which reduces principal by approximately $2,264.35 and brings the balance to approximately $149,040.21. They then apply the $6,000 bonus and the scheduled $1,000 roof payment, reducing the balance to approximately $142,040.21.

The tracked roof balance had fallen to $7,000 after the first two scheduled payments. The $6,000 bonus and the third $1,000 payment eliminate the remaining amount. The roof draw is now fully repaid. The total HELOC balance of approximately $142,040.21 is lower than the balance before the repair, demonstrating that the couple continued making permanent progress while repaying the temporary borrowing.

The couple reviews the first nine months. The original balance was $168,000, and the current balance is approximately $142,040.21. The net principal reduction is approximately $25,959.79. Their original year-end target was a $24,000 reduction, so they are already about $1,959.79 beyond the full-year goal.

However, James and Olivia do not immediately use the restored credit. They still have three months remaining and decide to establish a stretch target of $136,000. The difference between the current balance and the stretch target is approximately $6,040.21. Achieving it requires an average principal reduction of approximately $2,013.40 per month.

During the tenth month, the rate increases from 9.80 percent to 10.30 percent. Simplified monthly interest on the $142,040.21 balance becomes approximately $1,219.18. Their regular $3,500 payment reduces principal by approximately $2,280.82, bringing the balance to approximately $139,759.39.

In the eleventh month, simplified interest on the lower balance is approximately $1,199.60. Another $3,500 payment reduces principal by approximately $2,300.40, bringing the balance to approximately $137,458.99. The rate increase raises the interest cost, but the lower balance allows the couple to continue making meaningful principal progress.

During the twelfth month, simplified interest on $137,458.99 is approximately $1,179.86. The couple pays $3,500, reducing principal by approximately $2,320.14. The estimated year-end balance becomes approximately $135,138.85.

James and Olivia began the year owing $168,000 and end owing approximately $135,138.85. Their net principal reduction is approximately $32,861.15. They exceed their original $24,000 goal by approximately $8,861.15 and finish about $861.15 below the revised stretch target of $136,000.

The gross payment total does not equal this principal reduction. They made twelve regular payments of $3,500, totaling $42,000. They made two additional $1,000 roof payments, one additional $1,000 roof payment in the bonus month, a $10,000 business-distribution payment, and a $6,000 bonus payment. Their total cash transferred to the HELOC was therefore substantial.

Part of those payments covered interest, and part was offset by redraws. The planned tax redraw was $4,000, and the roof draw was $9,000, creating total draws of $13,000. The account's activity was much greater than the final $32,861.15 principal reduction. The ending balance provides the clearest measurement of permanent net progress.

The couple calculates approximate annual interest savings based on the difference between the opening and closing balances at the ending rate of 10.30 percent. The $32,861.15 principal reduction multiplied by 10.30

percent produces estimated future annual interest savings of approximately $3,384.70 if the balance and rate remain unchanged. Dividing by twelve produces approximate monthly savings of $282.06.

At the beginning of the year, the $168,000 balance at 10.30 percent would produce simplified monthly interest of approximately $1,442. At the ending balance of approximately $135,138.85, simplified monthly interest is approximately $1,159.94. The difference confirms the estimated monthly savings of about $282.

The couple's available credit also rises. At the beginning of the year, the $240,000 credit limit minus the $168,000 balance produced approximately $72,000 of available credit. At year-end, the credit limit minus the approximate $135,138.85 balance produces approximately $104,861.15 of available credit.

James and Olivia do not regard the $104,861.15 as money available for unrestricted spending. Their internal balance ceiling for the next year is $140,000. With a current balance of approximately $135,138.85, their self-approved borrowing capacity is only about $4,861.15. This limit protects the year's progress.

Their annual review also considers liquidity. The couple began the year with $48,000 in cash reserves and ends with $51,000. The HELOC balance declined while cash reserves increased by $3,000. This confirms that the principal reduction was not achieved by draining the protected reserve.

They calculate the redraw ratio using the $13,000 of total draws and the approximate gross principal applied during the year. If gross principal payments totaled approximately $45,861.15 before subtracting the $13,000 of redraws, the redraw ratio was approximately 28.35 percent. The remaining 71.65 percent of gross principal activity produced permanent net reduction.

The ratio helps the couple evaluate future behavior. The roof and tax draws were planned and supported by specific repayment sources, but they still consumed part of the principal paid during the year. James and Olivia decide that the next year's redraw ratio should remain below 20 percent unless a significant emergency occurs.

They also review the reason for each draw. The $4,000 tax draw returned money that had been placed temporarily into the line, while the $9,000 roof draw funded a necessary repair and was repaid within the scheduled period. No draw was used for routine consumption, entertainment, or an unsupported purchase. The behavioral review confirms that the account followed the household's rules.

The example demonstrates why a HELOC should be evaluated through net results rather than gross activity. James and Olivia paid significant amounts into the account, temporarily deposited tax money, made a necessary repair draw, repaid that draw, experienced a rate increase, preserved cash, and still exceeded the principal target. Their internal ledger made each movement understandable.

A borrower who does not maintain this record may see a constantly changing balance without knowing whether the strategy is working. By recording opening balances, interest, payments, draws, temporary deposits, permanent reductions, cash reserves, and targets, the homeowner can distinguish useful flexibility from uncontrolled borrowing.

The true measure of success is not the number of payments made or the amount of credit restored. It is the amount of principal that remains eliminated after all redraws have occurred, combined with the household's

ability to preserve adequate cash. James and Olivia's ending balance, lower interest exposure, protected reserves, and stricter internal ceiling demonstrate measurable progress that can be continued into the next year.

Chapter 8

Building a Complete HELOC Paydown, Redraw, and Exit Plan

A HELOC paydown-and-redraw strategy becomes most effective when every individual decision supports a defined long-term outcome. Making extra payments, lowering the average daily balance, preserving cash, controlling redraws, and monitoring variable rates are valuable practices, but they should not operate as isolated techniques. The homeowner needs a complete plan that explains where the HELOC balance is today, where it should be at specific future dates, when borrowing remains permissible, and how the account will eventually be repaid or converted into a manageable obligation.

The purpose of an exit plan is not necessarily to close the HELOC immediately. A homeowner may have valid reasons to keep the line open during the draw period, particularly when income is irregular, major property expenses are possible, or access to short-term capital provides meaningful flexibility. The exit plan determines how that access will be preserved without allowing the debt to remain indefinitely. It creates a gradual transition from active borrowing capacity to lower principal, restricted redrawing, and eventual repayment.

The plan begins with an accurate financial starting point. The homeowner should record the HELOC credit limit, current principal balance, available credit, current rate, contractual margin, rate ceiling, required payment, draw-period expiration date, repayment-period term, and projected payment after conversion. This information defines the structure within which every future decision must be made.

The borrower should then identify the amount of cash currently available and divide it according to purpose. Money required for current bills, known upcoming expenses, taxes, business obligations, and the emergency reserve is not surplus. Only cash remaining after these obligations have been protected should be considered for HELOC principal reduction. This prevents the exit plan from beginning with an oversized payment that must soon be reversed.

The cash-reserve floor should be written into the plan as a dollar amount rather than described vaguely. A homeowner who decides to keep "enough savings" may repeatedly change the definition depending on the latest financial pressure. A written floor of $40,000, for example, provides a clear boundary. Principal payments can continue while cash remains above that level, and they can pause when reserves fall below it.

The reserve floor should be supported by a calculation. The borrower may select four, six, or more months of essential expenses and add money for insurance deductibles, property repairs, medical needs, or business volatility. The result should reflect the household's actual risk rather than a general recommendation. A homeowner dependent on irregular business income may need a larger reserve than a household with two stable salaries.

Once liquidity is protected, the homeowner establishes the final balance objective. This may be complete repayment before the draw period ends, a specific balance that can be comfortably amortized, or a lower balance that can be refinanced responsibly. The objective should be based on affordable payments and long-term cash flow rather than on the maximum amount the lender permits the borrower to owe.

If the borrower does not expect to eliminate the balance before conversion, the target should be calculated from the desired repayment-period payment. Suppose the homeowner wants the future payment to remain below $1,500 per month and expects a fifteen-year repayment term. The borrower can estimate the balance that would produce that payment at a stress-tested rate. This calculation provides a practical ending-balance target.

The target balance should be lower than the amount that appears affordable at the current rate. Because HELOC rates are often variable, a plan based only on today's rate may become inadequate after an increase. Testing a rate two to four percentage points higher can reveal whether the target contains enough protection. The contractual maximum rate may also be considered if it represents a plausible risk.

After choosing the final target, the homeowner divides the required reduction into annual, quarterly, and monthly milestones. If the current balance is $180,000 and the target is $100,000 four years from now, the borrower must achieve a net reduction of $80,000. Dividing by four produces an average annual goal of $20,000, while dividing by 48 months produces an average monthly goal of approximately $1,666.67.

The word net is essential. A monthly principal payment of $1,666.67 will not produce the planned result if the borrower also redraws $10,000 every six months. The milestone must be measured after every redraw. The borrower can still use the line, but each draw must include a repayment schedule that returns the account to the planned balance path.

The homeowner should establish two balance limits. The first is the lender's credit limit, which represents the maximum borrowing capacity under the agreement. The second is the household's internal ceiling, which is the highest balance the borrower permits regardless of lender availability. The internal ceiling should begin near the current balance and decline as the exit plan advances.

A borrower with a $250,000 HELOC limit and a current balance of $150,000 might establish an initial internal ceiling of $160,000. After one year, the ceiling could fall to $140,000, then to $120,000, and eventually to $100,000. Even if principal payments restore more than $100,000 of lender-approved credit, the declining ceiling prevents the line from returning to its original balance.

The plan should specify approved redraw categories. Critical home repairs, necessary medical expenses, temporary business needs supported by documented receivables, and other significant obligations may qualify. Discretionary travel, routine consumption, entertainment, cosmetic projects, and spending that exceeds the monthly budget should ordinarily be excluded.

Every approved draw should identify the amount, purpose, repayment source, repayment deadline, and effect on the balance milestone. If a draw pushes the account above its scheduled balance, the borrower should determine how quickly the excess will be eliminated. A draw without a defined repayment source should not be approved merely because available credit exists.

The exit plan should include a redraw phaseout schedule. During the early years, the homeowner may allow carefully controlled borrowing that can be repaid within twelve months. As the draw period shortens, permitted repayment periods should become shorter. During the final year, the borrower may prohibit every nonemergency draw and treat additional principal payments as permanent.

This gradual restriction recognizes that available credit becomes less dependable as the conversion date approaches. A borrower should not pay money into the line during the final months with the assumption that it can be retrieved after the draw period ends. Cash needed for future expenses should remain outside the HELOC.

Payment timing should support the exit plan. True surplus can be applied after each paycheck, business distribution, commission, bonus, or rental deposit rather than waiting until the end of the month. Earlier payments may lower the average daily balance and reduce interest. The homeowner should still protect the reserve floor and fund every obligation due before the next income deposit.

The plan may use both fixed and percentage-based payments. A fixed monthly principal goal creates dependable progress, while a percentage rule captures irregular income. A homeowner might commit to $1,500 of principal per month plus 40 percent of every bonus, commission, or business distribution above the reserve requirement. This structure provides a minimum pace and an opportunity to accelerate.

The required total payment must include both interest and the planned principal reduction. If monthly interest is approximately $1,200 and the principal target is $1,500, the borrower must pay approximately $2,700. Sending only $1,500 would cover interest first and reduce principal by only about $300. This mistake can delay the exit plan for years.

The homeowner should update the total payment whenever the rate changes. If interest rises from $1,200 to $1,450, the payment must rise from approximately $2,700 to $2,950 to maintain the same $1,500 principal reduction. If the household cannot increase the payment, redraws should be restricted and the timeline should be reevaluated immediately.

A rate-trigger system can make these responses automatic. A one-percentage-point increase may lead to a higher monthly payment. A two-percentage-point increase may suspend nonessential draws. A three-percentage-point increase may activate a principal payment from the rate-defense fund or prompt a comparison of fixed-rate alternatives. Predetermined actions reduce the risk of delaying a decision while interest accumulates.

The homeowner should establish a rule for windfalls. Tax refunds, bonuses, asset-sale proceeds, inheritance, business distributions, and other irregular funds can accelerate the plan, but not every dollar should automatically be sent to the HELOC. Taxes, reserves, and known expenses must be protected first. The remaining amount can be divided between principal reduction and other financial priorities.

A windfall allocation rule might direct 60 percent of true after-tax proceeds to the HELOC, 20 percent to cash reserves, and 20 percent to another goal. A borrower whose reserve is already fully funded may increase the HELOC percentage. The rule should be established before the money arrives so that the decision is not driven by immediate spending opportunities.

Other debts must be incorporated into the exit strategy. A high-rate credit card may deserve priority over additional HELOC principal, while a low-rate car loan may not. The borrower should compare rates, required payments, collateral risk, remaining terms, and the effect each debt has on household cash flow. Paying one obligation should strengthen the complete plan rather than merely shift debt from one account to another.

Using the HELOC to consolidate unsecured debt requires additional caution. A lower rate may reduce interest, but unsecured debt becomes debt secured by the home. The strategy works only if the original cards remain paid down and the transferred balance is repaid according to a defined schedule. If the cards are reused, the household may end with both a larger HELOC and new credit card balances.

The homeowner should maintain a monthly HELOC review. The review records the opening balance, interest rate, interest charged, fees, total payments, principal paid, new draws, ending balance, available credit, cash reserve, internal ceiling, and remaining draw period. These figures reveal whether the line remains on the planned path.

A quarterly review should examine the broader assumptions. The borrower should confirm whether income remains stable, expenses have changed, the reserve floor remains appropriate, rates have increased, property repairs are expected, and the projected repayment-period payment remains affordable. Annual targets can be adjusted when circumstances change, but adjustments should not become excuses for avoiding principal reduction.

If the balance falls behind the milestone, the homeowner should calculate the exact shortfall. Suppose the scheduled balance is $130,000 but the actual balance is $136,000. The borrower is $6,000 behind. If six months remain before the annual target date, an additional $1,000 of net principal reduction per month is required to close the gap.

The plan should include a recovery procedure. The homeowner may suspend discretionary draws, direct a larger percentage of irregular income to principal, reduce optional spending, use cash above the reserve floor, or extend the target cautiously. The response should address the reason for the shortfall. If excessive spending created the gap, increasing payments without changing spending may produce only temporary improvement.

The plan should also define when HELOC use has become unsuccessful. Warning signs include a balance that rises for several consecutive quarters, repeated draws for ordinary expenses, interest charges that consume the entire planned payment, cash reserves below the protected floor, or dependence on obtaining a new HELOC to repay the existing one. These conditions require a change in strategy.

A borrower may need to stop redrawing entirely. The revolving structure is useful only when it supports disciplined capital management. If restored availability repeatedly encourages spending, a fixed repayment structure may better support the household. The homeowner can voluntarily stop using the line even while it remains open.

Refinancing may become part of the exit plan, but it should not be treated as guaranteed. The borrower may compare a fixed-rate home equity loan, first-mortgage refinance, personal loan, or fixed-rate HELOC conversion. The analysis should include closing costs, repayment term, monthly payment, total interest, collateral, and the effect of extending the debt.

A lower monthly payment is not sufficient evidence that refinancing is beneficial. If a $100,000 HELOC balance with ten years remaining is refinanced over 30 years, the payment may fall while total interest increases significantly. The borrower should compare the cost over the intended payoff period, not merely the lender's minimum schedule.

The homeowner should prepare credit and documentation well before pursuing a replacement loan. Income, credit scores, property value, combined loan-to-value ratio, and lender guidelines may affect approval. Self-employed borrowers should maintain organized bank statements, tax records, profit-and-loss statements, and other relevant documents. The exit plan should remain workable even if refinancing is unavailable.

Selling the property may also be a legitimate exit method when it supports the homeowner's broader goals. The HELOC and first mortgage would ordinarily be paid from sale proceeds before the owner receives the remaining equity. The homeowner should estimate selling costs, mortgage payoffs, taxes, moving expenses, and the cost of replacement housing before relying on this option.

Complete repayment may be the preferred outcome for many borrowers. Once the balance reaches zero, the homeowner must decide whether to keep the unused line open or formally close it. Keeping it open may preserve access during the remaining draw period, but annual fees, inactivity rules, early closure provisions, lender restrictions, and behavioral temptation should be considered.

If the line is kept open after reaching zero, the homeowner should retain strict redraw rules and a very low internal ceiling. A zero balance does not transform the credit line into savings. Any future draw creates new debt secured by the home. The borrower should maintain cash reserves even when the full credit limit appears available.

If the account is closed, the homeowner should request confirmation and verify the treatment of the lien according to the lender's procedures. Closing the account may involve additional documentation or recording steps. The borrower should also review whether an early closure fee or reimbursement of waived closing costs applies.

A successful exit plan should strengthen the homeowner's entire financial position. The HELOC balance declines, interest exposure falls, available equity increases, cash reserves remain protected, and future payments become more manageable. The plan should not achieve a zero balance while leaving the household without cash, carrying higher-cost debt, or facing unfunded obligations.

Behavioral discipline remains central to the plan. The mathematics may show that early payments save interest, but the savings occur only when the homeowner does not redraw the principal unnecessarily. Available credit can create a feeling of abundance that is not supported by income or cash. Written rules counter that feeling by assigning every dollar of borrowing a purpose and repayment deadline.

The homeowner should view restored availability as a preserved option rather than a financial reward. Paying down $25,000 and restoring $25,000 of credit does not create a new $25,000 spending allowance. The financial gain is the lower balance, lower interest, and increased flexibility. Using the entire restored amount without a compelling purpose reverses the gain.

The final stage of the plan should become increasingly simple. Redraws decline, temporary paydowns become permanent, the internal ceiling approaches the target balance, and the household becomes accustomed to making principal-and-interest payments. By the time the draw period ends, the borrower should know exactly how the remaining balance will be handled.

The complete HELOC strategy can therefore be summarized through coordinated decisions. Cash reserves protect the household, surplus payments reduce the balance, early payment timing lowers the average daily balance, redraw rules preserve progress, rate triggers manage uncertainty, monthly reviews measure results, and the exit date keeps the plan moving toward a final outcome.

A HELOC can be a useful source of capital, but its revolving structure should not become a permanent borrowing cycle. The homeowner should retain access only as long as that access supports the larger financial plan.

The ultimate objective is not to maintain the highest possible credit availability. It is to preserve choices while steadily reducing the amount owed against the home.

When a borrower combines flexibility with a clear exit, the HELOC becomes a controlled financial instrument rather than an open-ended obligation. The homeowner knows how much cash must remain protected, how much principal must be paid, which draws are permitted, how those draws will be repaid, and what balance must be reached before the draw period ends. That level of control allows home equity to remain a source of strength rather than becoming a continuing source of financial pressure.

Practical Math Example: Comparing a Disciplined Four-Year Exit Plan With Minimum Payments and Continued Redraws

Consider homeowners Robert and Melissa, who have a HELOC with a $275,000 credit limit and an outstanding balance of $190,000. The current variable interest rate is 10.20 percent, and four years remain in the draw period. When the draw period ends, the balance will be amortized over fifteen years. Robert and Melissa want to preserve limited access to capital while reducing the balance to no more than $100,000 before conversion.

At the current $190,000 balance and 10.20 percent rate, simplified annual interest is approximately $19,380. Dividing by twelve produces a monthly interest estimate of approximately $1,615. Because the current minimum payment is primarily interest-only, paying approximately $1,615 per month would leave the principal balance near $190,000.

Robert and Melissa's target requires a net principal reduction of $90,000 over 48 months. Dividing $90,000 by 48 produces an average required principal reduction of $1,875 per month. At the initial interest estimate of

$1,615, the couple would need to pay approximately $3,490 during the first month to cover interest and meet the principal target.

They decide to round the total monthly payment to $3,500. During the first month, approximately $1,615 covers interest, and approximately $1,885 reduces principal. The ending balance falls from $190,000 to approximately $188,115. As the balance declines, the interest portion of the fixed payment should gradually fall if the rate remains unchanged, allowing more than $1,885 to reach principal.

The couple has $92,000 in cash. Their essential household expenses total approximately $9,000 per month. Because part of Robert's income is commission-based, they establish a six-month emergency reserve of $54,000. They also set aside $8,000 for insurance deductibles and known home expenses, plus a $5,000 checking buffer. Their total protected cash is therefore $67,000.

Subtracting the $67,000 protected amount from their $92,000 total cash produces $25,000 of possible surplus. Robert and Melissa decide to make an initial $15,000 principal payment and retain the other $10,000 as a rate-defense and opportunity buffer. The HELOC balance falls immediately from $190,000 to $175,000.

At the new $175,000 balance and 10.20 percent rate, simplified monthly interest falls to approximately $1,487.50. Their fixed $3,500 payment now directs approximately $2,012.50 toward principal during the first full month after the lump-sum reduction. The initial payment saves approximately $127.50 per month in interest at the current rate.

Robert and Melissa establish an internal balance ceiling of $185,000 for the first year. Although the lender shows approximately $100,000 of available credit after the initial payment, the couple permits only $10,000 of additional borrowing. Approved draws must be necessary, remain below the ceiling, and have a repayment source that can eliminate the draw within twelve months.

During the first year, the couple continues paying $3,500 per month. Using a simplified estimate that accounts for gradually declining interest, they reduce principal by approximately $25,000 through monthly payments. Combined with the initial $15,000 lump-sum payment, the balance falls from $190,000 to approximately $150,000 by the end of the first year.

At a $150,000 balance and 10.20 percent rate, simplified monthly interest is approximately $1,275. The fixed $3,500 payment would now direct approximately $2,225 toward principal during the next month. Their available credit rises to approximately $125,000, but their internal ceiling for the second year falls from $185,000 to $160,000.

Robert and Melissa calculate their first-year interest savings. If the balance had remained at $190,000, simplified annual interest at 10.20 percent would have been $19,380. Because the balance declined throughout the year, their actual simplified interest would be lower. Using an approximate average balance of $168,000 for the year, estimated interest is about $17,136. The first-year savings compared with maintaining the original balance are approximately $2,244.

During the second year, the HELOC rate increases from 10.20 percent to 11.20 percent. At the $150,000 balance, simplified monthly interest becomes approximately $1,400. If the couple maintains the $3,500 payment, approximately $2,100 reaches principal during the first month at the new rate.

The higher rate increases their interest cost, but the lower balance limits the effect. If they still owed $190,000, simplified monthly interest at 11.20

percent would be approximately $1,773.33. Their principal reduction therefore saves approximately $373.33 per month compared with carrying the original balance at the higher rate.

The rate increase activates their first trigger. Robert and Melissa apply $5,000 from the $10,000 rate-defense buffer to the HELOC. The balance falls from approximately $150,000 to $145,000 before the second year's regular paydown. At 11.20 percent, this payment reduces simplified monthly interest by approximately $46.67.

Six months into the second year, the couple needs $8,000 for a necessary plumbing repair. The draw passes their rules because it protects the property, remains below the $160,000 internal ceiling, and has a repayment source. Melissa expects a documented $5,000 net bonus in three months, and the household can pay an additional $1,000 per month for three months.

Before the draw, assume their regular payments have reduced the balance from $145,000 to approximately $132,000. The $8,000 draw increases it to approximately $140,000, which remains below the internal ceiling. At 11.20 percent, the draw initially adds approximately $74.67 to monthly interest.

Over the next three months, Robert and Melissa pay the normal $3,500 plus an additional $1,000 per month. The three additional payments reduce the repair obligation by $3,000. When Melissa receives the $5,000 bonus, she applies it to the HELOC and eliminates the remaining repair balance. The draw returns to zero within the planned period.

By the end of the second year, their regular payments and rate-trigger contribution reduce the total HELOC balance to approximately $118,000. The plumbing repair was completed, repaid, and prevented from becoming permanent debt. The couple lowers its third-year internal ceiling to $125,000.

At the $118,000 balance and 11.20 percent rate, simplified monthly interest is approximately $1,101.33. Their $3,500 payment can now direct approximately $2,398.67 toward principal during the first month of the third year. Compared with the original $1,615 monthly interest estimate, their current interest is approximately $513.67 lower despite the rate having increased by one percentage point.

During the third year, Robert's commission income declines temporarily. The household can maintain the cash-reserve floor and required bills, but paying $3,500 every month becomes difficult. The couple reduces the total HELOC payment to $3,000 for four months rather than using new draws to preserve the previous payment amount.

At the approximate $118,000 balance and 11.20 percent rate, the first month's interest is about $1,101.33. A $3,000 payment still reduces principal by approximately $1,898.67. The slower payment remains above the original average target of $1,875 in net monthly principal reduction.

After four months, Robert's income recovers. The couple resumes its $3,500 payment and directs 40 percent of the next large commission to the HELOC. Robert receives a $15,000 after-tax commission above the normal budget, and the allocation rule directs $6,000 toward principal.

Through regular payments and the $6,000 commission allocation, the HELOC balance falls to approximately $88,000 by the end of the third year. The couple reaches the original $100,000 final target one year early. Their internal ceiling for the final year is reduced to $95,000, permitting only $7,000 of self-approved emergency borrowing.

At a balance of $88,000 and an 11.20 percent rate, simplified monthly interest is approximately $821.33. A $3,500 payment would direct approximately $2,678.67 toward principal during the next month. Robert and Melissa could reduce their payment, but they decide to continue the same amount while income remains stable.

The draw period now has one year remaining, so the couple enters its redraw phaseout. All nonemergency draws are prohibited. Money needed for known expenses remains in cash, and every additional HELOC payment is treated as permanent because future redraw access will soon end.

During the final year, the rate rises again to 12.20 percent. At the $88,000 balance, simplified monthly interest becomes approximately $894.67. If the balance were still $190,000, monthly interest at 12.20 percent would be approximately $1,931.67. Their lower balance protects them from more than $1,000 of monthly interest exposure.

The second rate trigger allows them to consider using the remaining $5,000 rate-defense buffer. After reviewing the reserve and upcoming expenses, they determine that cash remains sufficient and apply the $5,000 to principal. The HELOC balance falls from approximately $88,000 to $83,000.

At a balance of $83,000 and a 12.20 percent rate, simplified monthly interest is approximately $843.83. Their $3,500 payment initially reduces principal by approximately $2,656.17. Continuing the payment throughout the final year lowers the balance rapidly.

Using a conservative simplified estimate, Robert and Melissa reduce principal by another $33,000 during the final year. The balance at the end of the draw period is approximately $50,000. This is $140,000 below the original $190,000 balance and $50,000 below their initial target.

If the $50,000 balance converts into a fifteen-year repayment period at 12.20 percent, the approximate principal-and-interest payment would be about $609 per month. Because Robert and Melissa are accustomed to paying $3,500, they have considerable flexibility. They may continue making larger payments and eliminate the remaining balance much sooner than the lender's fifteen-year schedule.

If they paid only the approximate $609 required amount for fifteen years, total payments would equal approximately $109,620. Subtracting the $50,000 principal produces approximately $59,620 of repayment-period interest. However, maintaining a $3,500 payment would repay the remaining balance far more quickly and dramatically reduce the total interest.

The couple compares this disciplined plan with an alternative minimum-payment-and-redraw approach. Under the alternative, they would make only interest payments during the four remaining draw years and use available credit for a $20,000 renovation, $12,000 of vacations and discretionary purchases, and $8,000 of routine expenses during weaker income months.

These draws would add $40,000 to the original $190,000 balance, producing an ending balance of approximately $230,000 before considering any capitalized fees or unpaid interest. At the final 12.20 percent rate, simplified monthly interest on $230,000 would be approximately $2,338.33.

When the $230,000 balance enters a fifteen-year repayment schedule at 12.20 percent, the approximate principal-and-interest payment would be about $2,800 per month. In contrast, the disciplined plan's $50,000 ending balance produces an approximate payment of only $609 per month. The difference is approximately $2,191 per month.

The alternative plan also leaves substantially less equity. If the home is worth $650,000 and the first mortgage balance is $300,000, total secured debt under the disciplined plan would be $350,000, consisting of the $300,000 first mortgage and $50,000 HELOC. The combined loan-to-value ratio would be approximately 53.85 percent.

Under the minimum-payment-and-redraw plan, total secured debt would be $530,000, consisting of the $300,000 first mortgage and $230,000 HELOC. The combined loan-to-value ratio would be approximately 81.54 percent. The disciplined plan therefore preserves an additional $180,000 of equity compared with the alternative balance.

The $180,000 difference includes the $140,000 principal reduction achieved by the disciplined plan and the $40,000 of additional draws avoided. At the final 12.20 percent rate, $180,000 of additional debt would generate approximately $21,960 of annual interest, or $1,830 per month, before considering amortization.

Robert and Melissa also compare their available cash. They finish the four-year plan with a $70,000 reserve after accounting for household changes and known expenses. They did not reach the lower HELOC balance by eliminating liquidity. Their preserved cash means that they enter the repayment period without depending on a replacement credit line.

The couple's success is not the result of one unusually large payment. It comes from coordinating an initial surplus payment, fixed monthly payments, declining internal ceilings, a rate-defense fund, controlled redraws, bonus allocations, temporary payment adjustments, and a final-year redraw phaseout. Every part of the plan supports the same exit objective.

The practical comparison shows how differently the same HELOC can develop over four years. One approach treats the line as a managed source of temporary capital and steadily reduces the balance. The other makes minimum payments, uses restored and unused credit for additional spending, and reaches conversion with more debt than it had at the beginning.

The disciplined strategy still allows flexibility. Robert and Melissa complete a necessary plumbing repair and temporarily reduce their monthly payment during weaker income months. Their plan is not rigid, but every adjustment remains within established limits. The repair has a repayment source, the lower payment still reduces principal, and the cash reserve remains protected.

Their final balance of approximately $50,000 gives them several choices. They can follow the scheduled repayment plan, continue paying $3,500 and eliminate the debt quickly, compare a fixed-rate option, or use a future windfall to pay the line in full. The minimum-payment alternative offers fewer choices because the much larger balance consumes more monthly income and equity.

The central lesson is that access to credit and freedom from debt can coexist only when the borrower maintains a clear direction. A HELOC can be paid down and selectively redrawn without losing control, but every draw must be temporary, every milestone must be measured after borrowing, and the internal balance ceiling must continue declining.

By the end of the plan, Robert and Melissa no longer measure success according to the amount of available credit. They measure it through the lower principal balance, reduced interest expense, preserved cash, affordable repayment payment, and increased home equity. Their HELOC remains a financial tool, but it no longer determines the direction of their household finances.

Summary and Conclusions

A home equity line of credit can provide homeowners with valuable financial flexibility, but that flexibility must be managed with a clear understanding of how the account works. A HELOC is not simply another installment loan with a fixed balance and predictable repayment schedule. During the draw period, it is generally a revolving line that allows the homeowner to borrow, repay principal, restore available credit, and borrow again. This structure can help a household manage irregular income, major expenses, property repairs, business needs, and temporary cash-flow gaps. At the same time, it can make it easy to remain in debt indefinitely if every principal payment is followed by another redraw.

The central lesson of this book is that a successful HELOC strategy must accomplish two objectives simultaneously. It must reduce the outstanding balance and the interest charged on that balance while preserving an appropriate amount of liquidity and future financial flexibility. Paying down the line as aggressively as possible may appear mathematically attractive, particularly when the rate is high, but the strategy can become dangerous if it leaves the household without sufficient cash. Available HELOC credit should never be treated as a complete replacement for money held in checking, savings, or another dependable reserve account.

A homeowner must begin by distinguishing among the credit limit, outstanding balance, and available credit. The credit limit represents the maximum amount the lender has approved under the account's terms. The outstanding balance is the amount currently owed, while available credit is generally the unused portion of the line. Available credit is not income, savings, or equity that has already been converted into personal wealth. It is additional borrowing capacity that may create interest and increase the amount secured by the home if it is used.

The cash-reserve floor provides the foundation for responsible paydown. Before applying surplus money to the HELOC, the homeowner should calculate essential monthly expenses, account for income stability, identify known upcoming obligations, and consider potential insurance deductibles, property repairs, medical costs, business needs, and family responsibilities. Money required for these purposes should remain protected. Only the amount above the reserve floor, operating buffer, and known obligations should ordinarily be considered true surplus.

The reserve floor makes long-term balance reduction more sustainable. A homeowner who sends too much cash to the HELOC may be forced to redraw the money when an emergency or irregular expense occurs. If the line has been frozen, reduced, or converted into repayment status, the money may not be available. The borrower might then turn to higher-cost credit cards, personal loans, missed payments, or the sale of investments. A reasonable reserve reduces the probability that an aggressive payment will create another financial problem.

Once the reserve has been protected, principal payments can be timed to reduce the average daily balance. Because many HELOCs calculate interest using daily balances, an earlier payment can produce more savings than the same payment made near the end of the billing cycle. Homeowners receiving regular salaries can coordinate payments with their paydays, while business owners and commission-based workers can apply verified surplus when larger deposits arrive. The purpose is to reduce the number of dollars generating interest and the number of days those dollars remain outstanding.

Payment timing should never override cash-flow safety. Money required for taxes, payroll, household bills, insurance, or another known obligation is not automatically available for permanent paydown. Temporary deposits may reduce interest while the money remains in the line, but they require careful planning. The borrower should record the amount, expected redraw date, purpose, and risk of losing access before temporarily applying assigned funds.

Every principal payment should be classified as either permanent or temporary. Permanent paydown represents money that the borrower intends to leave in the line and contributes directly to the long-term balance objective. Temporary paydown represents money that may be redrawn for a known expense. Both can lower interest, but only the permanent portion should be counted toward the final payoff or conversion target. This distinction prevents account activity from being mistaken for lasting progress.

Redrawing should be governed by written rules. The fact that principal repayment restores available credit does not mean the restored amount should be spent. An approved redraw should have a defined purpose, limited amount, identified repayment source, specific deadline, affordable payment, and clear relationship to the household's internal balance ceiling. If these conditions cannot be satisfied, the draw should ordinarily be delayed, reduced, or rejected.

The purpose of the draw matters because borrowing against the home carries consequences. Necessary property repairs, significant medical needs, carefully analyzed business expenses, and temporary income disruptions may justify HELOC use. Routine living costs, vacations, entertainment, cosmetic projects, and recurring budget shortages generally indicate that the household is using long-term secured debt to fund consumption. Repeatedly borrowing for normal expenses can turn a temporary cash-flow problem into a growing claim against the home.

Every redraw should have a repayment source before the money is borrowed. Monthly surplus income, documented receivables, a scheduled bonus, rental proceeds, an insurance reimbursement, or the planned sale of an asset may provide that source. A vague expectation that future income will improve is not sufficient. The borrower should calculate the monthly principal required to eliminate the draw by the chosen deadline and add that amount to the interest due.

Variable-rate risk must remain part of every decision. A HELOC rate may increase even when no additional money is borrowed. The larger the balance, the greater the effect of each rate adjustment. Permanent principal reduction acts as protection because the higher rate applies to fewer dollars. A borrower cannot control the index used to set the rate, but the borrower can influence the balance exposed to that index.

Stress testing helps the homeowner prepare for future changes. The current balance and every proposed redraw should be evaluated at the present rate and at one or more higher rates. If a draw is affordable only under today's payment, the plan may be too fragile. A rate-trigger system can establish automatic responses, such as increasing principal payments, suspending nonessential draws, using part of a rate-defense fund, or comparing fixed-rate alternatives when the rate reaches specific levels.

The homeowner should also establish an internal HELOC ceiling that is lower than the lender's credit limit. A lender may approve a $250,000 line, but the household may decide never to owe more than $140,000. As the balance declines, the internal ceiling should also decline. This prevents restored availability from becoming a new spending target and ensures that every stage of the strategy moves toward lower debt.

The end of the draw period must be treated as a firm financial deadline. When the draw period expires, access to additional funds may stop, and the outstanding balance may enter a principal-and-interest repayment schedule. A borrower accustomed to making interest-only payments can experience a significant payment increase even if the rate and balance remain unchanged. A rate increase before or after conversion can make the payment shock even greater.

Preparing for that transition requires identifying the expiration date, repayment term, projected payment, and target ending balance. A homeowner who does not expect to eliminate the line before conversion should determine which balance would produce an affordable principal-and-interest payment. That amount should become the final draw-period target, and the required reduction should be divided into annual, quarterly, and monthly milestones.

The borrower can begin practicing the future payment before it becomes mandatory. If the current interest-only payment is $1,200 and the projected repayment payment is $1,800, voluntarily paying $1,800 during the draw period allows the budget to adjust while the additional $600 reduces principal. As the balance declines, interest falls, more of the payment reaches principal, and the eventual required payment may become smaller.

Redraw permissions should become more restrictive as the end of the draw period approaches. Early in the plan, the homeowner may approve narrowly defined draws that can be repaid within twelve months. During the final years, repayment deadlines should become shorter. In the final year, nonemergency borrowing may need to stop entirely. Money paid into the line near conversion should increasingly be treated as permanent because future redraw access may disappear.

Measuring the strategy requires more than adding up total payments. The true result is the net change in principal after interest, fees, and every redraw have been considered. A homeowner may transfer $50,000 into the account during a year, but if $15,000 covers interest and $20,000 is redrawn, the net principal reduction is only $15,000. Gross payment activity can look impressive while producing limited permanent improvement.

A monthly HELOC review should record the opening balance, current rate, interest charged, fees, total payments, principal paid, new draws, ending balance, available credit, cash reserves, internal balance ceiling, and time remaining in the draw period. The ending balance should be compared with the prior month, the beginning of the year, and the planned target. These comparisons reveal whether the account is moving in the intended direction.

Quarterly and annual reviews provide a broader view. A single month may contain a large approved draw or irregular expense, but a multi-month review shows whether the balance returns to its previous path. If the balance rises over several consecutive periods, the homeowner must determine whether the cause is excessive borrowing, higher interest, inadequate payments, or a structural budget deficit.

The strongest HELOC exit plan coordinates all of these decisions. The homeowner establishes a reserve floor, determines the final target balance, creates monthly principal goals, times surplus payments efficiently, limits redraws, assigns repayment sources, prepares for higher rates, and gradually reduces the internal balance ceiling. The plan also explains how the remaining balance will be handled when the draw period ends.

Refinancing may eventually become part of the plan, but it should never be assumed. A replacement loan may depend on credit, income, property value, loan-to-value ratio, documentation, and future lender guidelines. A lower monthly payment can also conceal a longer repayment term and greater total interest. The existing plan should remain workable even if refinancing is unavailable.

Complete repayment may ultimately provide the greatest freedom, but the homeowner should decide whether to close the line or keep it open with a zero balance. Keeping the account open may preserve access during the remaining draw period, but it may also involve fees, restrictions, or behavioral temptation. Closing the line removes the ability to redraw but may require additional lender and lien-release procedures. The appropriate decision depends on the borrower's goals, discipline, and account terms.

The mathematics of HELOC management are important, but behavior determines whether the expected savings become real. A spreadsheet may demonstrate that early payments reduce interest, yet those savings disappear if the principal is repeatedly redrawn for unnecessary purchases. A strict system may be more valuable than a theoretically perfect strategy that the household cannot follow consistently.

Home equity represents years of mortgage payments, property ownership, maintenance, and financial commitment. Accessing that equity can support important needs and opportunities, but accessibility should never be confused with affordability. Every draw increases debt secured by the property, and every principal payment should move the homeowner toward a stronger position.

The most successful strategy does not necessarily eliminate the HELOC at the fastest possible speed. It reduces the balance at a sustainable pace while preserving necessary cash and preventing new borrowing from erasing progress. For one household, this may mean large principal payments and almost no redraws. For another, it may mean using seasonal income to reduce the balance and allowing narrowly controlled draws during predictable low-income periods.

The final measure of success is whether the homeowner finishes with less debt, lower interest exposure, stronger liquidity, greater equity, and an affordable path through the repayment period. Available credit may remain part of the plan, but it should function as a preserved option rather than a spending objective. The lower balance, not the larger borrowing capacity, is the true financial achievement.

A HELOC can provide flexibility without becoming a permanent cycle of borrowing when it is managed with discipline. Protect cash, reduce principal, make payments early when practical, redraw only for approved purposes, assign a repayment source to every draw, monitor rates, prepare for conversion, and measure net progress consistently. These principles allow homeowners to reduce interest while preserving responsible access to capital and keeping control of their home equity firmly connected to their long-term financial goals.

www.ingramcontent.com/pod-product-compliance
Lightning Source LLC
LaVergne TN
LVHW030726061126
851857LV00019B/2009